A Space Time Apocalypse

Anthony Fox

chipmunkapublishing
the mental health publisher

All rights reserved, no part of this publication may be reproduced by any means, electronic, mechanical photocopying, documentary, film or in any other format without prior written permission of the publisher.

> Published by
> Chipmunkapublishing
> United Kingdom

http://www.chipmunkapublishing.com

Copyright © **Anthony Fox 2019**

ISBN   978-1-78382-456-4

A Space Time Apocalypse

I thank family and friends for their encouragement during this project.

Anthony Fox

Chapter 1

Turn off the light and take a deep breath, it took thousands of years before humanity would know the secret that had been hidden for so long, but the time had come for the world to know. The word 'zombie' was not just a fictional characterisation in a Hollywood film or book, but a reality only 'Iron Smart' knew an artificially intelligent robot sent to earth on a final mission.

"We are entering the planet's gravity wave," said Iron Smart the alien commander.

As the alien spacecraft slowed and entered the Earth's upper atmosphere, the spacecraft immediately began searching the terrain for a suitable landing site. The spacecraft's internal computer system had selected a remote part of the 'Gobi' desert in Mongolia.

"Commander, we have safely landed and deployed the shield and now wait for your commands," said Shogi second in command under Iron Smart.

***

Meanwhile, Professor Aaron Mikovitz was just waking up from a bad dream as the sun began to rise. It was something his girlfriend Dr. Janet Taylor and colleague had said to him the night before at the South California Observatory, just think she had said, "If alien spacecraft get to us before we get to them their technology would be 'worlds apart' and could be deadly."

Aaron looked out from his bedroom window at the waning crescent moon as he sat at his desk. He couldn't get back to sleep and the next best was to be fully awake at his laptop that was digitally linked to the South California Observatory, which was a distraction he never tired of. Ever since, his time at university at the University of California Los Angles (UCLA) his hobby and career had coincided, which suited his personality and ambition.

Aaron was born in Los Angles, California, from Jewish immigrant parents, who had emigrated from Italy to America shortly before the Second World War. Aaron was the oldest of three siblings that didn't always see eye to eye. His younger brother and sister had the same dark features associated with Jews as Aaron had. Aaron was often irritated by some people who mistook his brown eyes, olive skin and jet black curly hair for an Arab person and not for his Jewish heritage. Although, most people who knew Aaron observed just another scientist with spectacles they didn't know he had an obsession like a couple in love, only, it was with the science of Near Earth Objects (NEOs) or asteroids, meteors and comets that he felt sure could one day threaten man's existence on planet Earth.

In Aaron's mind, he briefly wondered about the dream he had that had used flies as miniscule nano robots that secretly spied for the aliens. Biological or mechanical it made no difference the flies were as covert as flies around a jam pot. Except these flies spied for the alien force that had been observing our planet since the dawn of man. It was just a dream…

***

Later that morning, Professor Aaron Mikovitz and Dr. Janet Taylor were busy checking the overnight email alerts. These email alerts were sent by various observatories stationed around the world that were busy watching the night sky for near earth objects as part of the Global Eyes project set up by various governments. The Global Eyes project was setup to provide an early warning system from asteroids, meteors and comets potentially colliding with Earth.

"Take a look at this, Aaron."

As Aaron read the message on his computer terminal, he remembered his dream again.

"This shows it came down in the 'Gobi' desert, approximately 3.30 am local time. We have not had any damage or casualty reports from this area; so, it's more than likely another one of those upper atmospheric air explosions."

"Don't be quick to jump to assumptions, Janet. Remember, we are scientists that follow the evidence that leads us to the truth. Whatever that may be?" Aaron paused for a moment perplexed by what he saw on his computer terminal.

Aaron continued, "That's strange…"

"What's strange? Don't keep it to yourself, Aaron." Aaron was having trouble with what he could see and for a moment he recalled the dream again he had the night before.

As Aaron pulled up a series of reports from the computer screen; it made no sense to him or Janet. They were both puzzled at what they saw on their computer screens.

"It entered our atmosphere, but left no chemical trace, it must be a malfunction of the data recovery systems," Janet said as she tried to check other computer data systems on her computer terminal to verify the information. Janet felt aware that it could be an Unidentified Flying Object (UFO).

Dr Janet Taylor had been dating Aaron since meeting at UCLA and now they were working together at the South California Observatory. Janet was born in Baltimore, Maryland to parents that could trace their ancestors nearly back to the first settlers in the New World. She had a precocious ability to say what she felt. Taller than most girls with long flowing brunette hair and deep blue eyes, Janet, had a panache when dealing with other people in authority that most people accepted as complementary to her character.

"If that asteroid disintegrated in the Gobi, it must be there." Aaron said, as he checked and rechecked the data. "Asteroids don't do that!"

Perplexed at Aaron's statement, Janet asked, "What don't they do?"

"Slow down…"

Chapter 2

That morning, the global news broadcasts were speculating on the size of an object hitting the earth and why the authorities hadn't given a warning, even though the suspected asteroid had landed in an uninhabited region of the 'Gobi' desert in Mongolia. The nearest town or village was reported to be approximately 14o kilometres from the suspected debris area. The news broadcast also said the nearest village to the suspected landing was named after a granddaughter of the prophet Mohammed.

The village had only a sparse and somewhat nomadic population according to the Central Intelligence Agency (CIA) file displayed on Frank Santoli's computer screen. Frank Santoli now in his mid-forties had been a special agent for the CIA since leaving the navy. Although, unmarried, he did harbour thoughts about getting married one day, if he could find the right woman, he would often say to himself. His Italian good looks were inherited from his immigrant parents, who had emigrated from Italy to America after the Second World War. Born in the Bronx, New York in an Italian neighbourhood, he had to learn to fight from a young age growing up with two older brothers who were constantly picking fights.

As Frank stroked his bald head and noted the information on the computer screen in his mind, his commander was on the phone wanting an update.

"What have you got, Santoli?" Frank was busy compiling his thoughts before revealing to his senior commander his answer. He was still puzzled at what the data of his computer screen was showing. "I'm not sure, boss…?"

"What do you mean?" asked Michael Stubbs a section chief of the Central Intelligence Agency (CIA) based at Langley, Virginia over the secure phone line.

"It landed approximately 140 kilometres from a village called Ayisha, but, I think, we have a problem, either with the source data or another UFO has just entered our airspace and landed without clearance and notification," remarked Frank candidly with a sly grin on his face.

"Well, as soon as you know the better…you better get out there and find out what landed. Remember, this is a need to know mission with level one clearance." Stubbs was quick to terminate the call, as he had other assholes waiting to speak to him, which was his view for most of his staff. Stubbs often said that some of his staff were quick to judge him, but most never had the balls in front of their commander to put their money where their mouth was. It was the same subordinates that were waiting to speak to him on the other phone lines as he sat on the back seat of the limousine. Stubbs was observing the scene at ease inside of his chauffeur driven vehicle with his large torso spread across the seats. The black limousine was carefully making its way through the rush hour traffic as it made its way to the White House along 'Patriots' Avenue' renamed after the defeat of the enemies of the United States during the previous years fighting terrorism. Apart from the rain and the noise of the traffic the air conditioned interior provided a comfort Michael Stubbs had got used to. 'Power corrupts, but without it there is no light,' he used to say to himself and others when the occasion permitted.

***

The overnight flight from Langley, Air Force Base to Mongolia allowed Frank Santoli time to consider his options. He also had time to read the file again on the local asset. The local Mongolian operative was at Chinggis Khaan International Airport to greet Frank Santoli as he departed the CIA corporate jet.

"Hope you had a pleasant journey, Mr Santoli?"

Frank already knew everything to know about the local asset. He had already read the file on the local CIA operative at Langley, before leaving and while on the plane again. From the photo of Ahmed Khan in his file, Frank noticed the typical facial features of a local Mongolian man with dark brown eyes set close together with short dark hair neatly trimmed. He was taller than most Mongolians from the description in the file and could speak several languages, which would be useful on this mission, thought Frank. Frank always liked to be familiar with any local asset as much as possible.

"Yes, glad you pulled the right strings with the military here, Ahmed," said Frank as they shook hands.

"Have Langley briefed you?"

"No. Only that you requested a helicopter."

"Good. We are going as they say…asteroid or is it meteor hunting. I always get mixed up with the two." But, in Frank

Santoli's mind, he already knew the distinction between the two. What lands on earth are called meteors and what just miss the earth are the asteroids. The same objects just different terms were used to signify its context. Besides, he was just playing with words to see what his partner on this mission would say. As it happens, Frank recalled that Ahmed had kept quiet. Perhaps, there was always a chance that Ahmed didn't have a clue; he had considered this for a moment.

Ahmed Khan had been recruited into the CIA after leaving the Mongolian defence force. During his initial training as a CIA operative, Ahmed had stressed the preference to stay in the country where he was born. He had studied politics at university before joining the army where he had made many close friends.

"The helicopter is over there, ready and waiting," remarked Ahmed pointing to the silhouette of a helicopter on the far side of the airport. Frank quickly identified the helicopter from its black shadow on the horizon, which he assumed to be the Russian G147 Class. His training in the CIA had to be comprehensive and that included learning past and present military and commercial vehicles and air transport configurations from around the world.

"How far is the village called Ayisha from here and also how far is the suspected debris area from the asteroid that came down?" asked Frank, who already knew the distance he just wanted to test Ahmed on his skills of preparedness.

"About an hour to Ayisha, and then another hour perhaps, depending on weather conditions. The helicopter is under military control, so, we don't have a say on that score."

"You know this village then?" asked Frank intrigued to know how much Ahmed knew about the village.

"Yes, it's famous for many reasons," replied Ahmed.

"No time to waste, let's get going."

***

"Commander, there's an aircraft approaching."

Iron Smart the alien commander could see the aircraft on its computerized defence system. The alien spacecraft's automated computer system was already locked on and ready to take offensive action if it needed to.

"We are protected with our shield and cloaked invisible to their technology," said Iron Smart to his second in command Shogi.

"We will see what they do."

***

Frank Santoli had found the supposed debris area of the asteroid using the Global Positioning System (GPS) that use satellites to accurately pin point where an object could be found. The alien's spacecraft was invisible to Frank Santoli and Ahmed Khan as they surveyed the area from inside the helicopter as it flew over several times before landing in a clearing beside a sand dune. Frank and Ahmed were unaware that on the other side of the valley was the presence of the alien's spacecraft invisibly parked.

"According to my GPS coordinates we are in the exact area where the fallout from the asteroid hit," remarked Frank to Ahmed.

As Frank and Ahmed searched the area they could find no debris from an asteroid, perhaps, the computer data was wrong, Frank was thinking.

"Are we really looking for the remains of an asteroid?" asked Ahmed.

"I was wondering when you were going ask that," replied Frank with a sly grin across his face.

"No. An UFO crashed here somewhere or it landed. Well, that's what our computer tracking told us."

"How do you know it was an UFO?" asked Ahmed.

"Well, the simple answer is, asteroids don't slow down," replied Frank.

***

"It's getting late. We better get back and make an early start tomorrow," muttered Frank as the cold wind made conversation an effort.

"No problem. We have full use of the helicopter as long as we need it," replied Ahmed.

"Good. Tomorrow, I want to stop off at that village, Ayisha. And see if anyone there saw anything."

"Bit of a longshot isn't?" muttered Ahmed who was also feeling the effects of the cold wind on his body.

"Yes, but I like the odds." Frank for a minute, let his guard down and smiled like a contented baby.

"Have you found a place I can stay the night?" asked Frank over the noise of the helicopter as they made their way back to the airport.

"Yes, we are sharing a room at the airport hotel," shouted Ahmed over the noise of the rotating helicopter blades. "It's all arranged."

Frank just nodded his head and in the meantime made a mental check list of things he needed to ask Ahmed when they got back to the hotel. He was sure the CIA's tracking systems would be within a few meters of an UFO landing. There were only two possible outcomes, either the tracking systems malfunctioned somehow or the UFO had some sort of stealth technology, which made their spacecraft invisible to the naked eye, he mused.

Ever since the 1980's the CIA had had spy satellites as part of the Strategic Defence Initiative (SDI) often called the 'Star Wars' defence system, which meant that America could track anything and everything that could possibly pose a threat to the security of America and its allies. Frank Santoli's opinion was the UFO had landed, but was using stealth technology to hide its whereabouts. There was no visible wreckage, which meant a controlled landing and their mission unknown. Tomorrow, he would know for sure, he said to himself.

***

At the Chinggis Khaan International Airport hotel, Frank and Ahmed made the cautionary checks for electronic bugs before they settled in their room for the night. It was standard practice for any CIA operative on a mission. Sharing a room was typical CIA; always watching the pennies, Frank wasn't bothered as long as he could get some sleep and have a shower. Although it made sense; why divide your strength when you didn't have to. Frank was sure he had a doppelganger somewhere that has fleas because he was always scratching everywhere and he knew he didn't have fleas.

"Anything on the TV news about the asteroid, Ahmed?" asked Frank.

"No, only they are not sure where it landed," replied Ahmed.

"It seems a local goat herder from Ayisha saw something. His name is Abu Bactu. He said, he saw something, but was drinking at the time, so he isn't sure or that reliable."

"Good, tomorrow, we need to find this man and find out what he saw before he tells everyone and there's a media circus. And if need be silence him," said Frank gazing into Ahmed eyes.

"Is that really necessary?" asked Ahmed.

"Well, it comes down to this. Would you rather have a national secret blasted out and cause a panic amongst the world or the silence of one person. This job is not about being nice it's about being professional, besides after we talk to him and the offer of some money then I'm sure you will not have to do the other thing." explained Frank calmly like it wasn't a big deal to quietly retire someone if they needed to.

When it came to using deadly force the prime objective and the difference between the local assets and a CIA agent were worlds apart. The CIA had a pecking order like any other organization and local assets were way down the cherry tree. Local assets were expendable and agents were not. Frank knew this and Ahmed knew as well, even if Ahmed needed reminding.

"Tell me what you know about the goat herder's village, called Ayisha?" asked Frank.

"A wealthy Muslim nomadic trader, who made his wealth trading wool and other goods named one of his daughters after the great granddaughter of the prophet Mohammed. Ayisha was reported to be a real beauty and many merchants and traders would travel many days just to see her and try to convince her father that they should be the one to marry Ayisha. With so many suitors Ayisha's father devised a plan."

Pausing for a moment before continuing, Ahmed asked, "Do you want to hear the full story, because it will take some time?"

"Yes, go on. You have me hooked. Frank was like a fish on a fishing line just waiting to be reeled in. But, before you do I will order some food," replied Frank.

"Okay, I will start. Ayisha's father was a shrewd business man and a devout Muslim. The whole family was Muslim, so it was natural that anyone marring his daughter would have to convert to Islam before they could marry Ayisha. This would also reduce the number of suitable suitors able to marry Ayisha," said Ahmed.

"Was there many religions competing for the inhabitants of Mongolia back then?" asked Frank who was intrigued to know the answer.

"Yes. The village started out as a trading post during the reign of Genghis Khan, who tolerated many religions during his reign, as did the Mongol dynasty that followed him," said Ahmed. Ahmed went on to explain that Genghis Khan who was known as the 'King of Kings' died in 1227, but even today Mongolians consider him the founder of Mongolia. Ahmed kept one eye on Frank as he relaxed laid out on the bed and one eye on the hotel bedroom door. He didn't feel as relaxed as Frank because he knew the risks working for the CIA.

Just then they heard a knock at the door; it was the porter with their food and refreshments. Frank gave the trolley a once over with the electronic bug detector and was satisfied there was no hidden devices before tucking into the food.

"Now, we are watered and fed, continue," remarked Frank.

"Ayisha's father had whittled the choice for Ayisha down to three candidates; one was a Jew and one was a Christian and the third a Muslim. The Jew and the Christian would have to convert to Islam before marrying Ayisha if they were chosen," said Ahmed as he continued with the story of Ayisha.

"Each of the three suitors would present a gift to Ayisha and explain why they chose their particular gift. The following day the three arrived at Ayisha's father's tent ready to present their gifts and tell their story," said Ahmed who had a smile like a child waiting for candy to eat.

As Ahmed looked at Frank he had already fallen asleep. Frank would have to wait for another day to hear what happened next in Ayisha's story. Ahmed composed his thoughts for the coming day and he too was quick to fall asleep.

***

Meanwhile, Professor Aaron Mikovitz and Dr. Janet Taylor had arrived at Chinggis Khaan airport situated close the capital Ulaanbaatar, Mongolia via a link from Moscow. The airport was named after Genghis Khan the legendary founder of Mongolia. The overnight flight from Los Angeles to Moscow had been uneventful apart from a child who had been sick a couple of rows in front of them, but the smell of sickness lingered for most of the duration of the flight, which made Arron feel sick for much of the flight. He was glad to be settling in a room for the night at the airport hotel. Janet had also booked a room only a couple doors down the corridor from Arron's room although they intended to sleep together. They figured it was best their employers were kept in the dark about their relationship.

In the hotel restaurant Arron and Janet were discussing their plans for the following day. They planned to charter a helicopter to the Global Positioning System (GPS) coordinates of the asteroid debris area; although they didn't believe it was an asteroid.

"You still believe it wasn't a meteor that landed in the desert?" asked Janet.

"All our computer systems cannot be wrong; otherwise, we'd be wasting our time here and the government's money looking for a meteor. Exciting as that may be," remarked Arron with a broad smile as if he already knew the answer to Janet's question.

"An UFO, it's possible."

"Anything is possible. Science is a challis full of opportunity," remarked Arron. It was a sentence he often used to describe his beliefs to friends and associates.

"Oh, by the way, if we get approached by the press; just say we're looking for the debris from an asteroid etc. Don't mention anything about an UFO." Aaron spent several minutes lecturing Janet on the potential fallout and media frenzy if they announced to the world that an UFO had landed. It was better to stay silent and let the world keep on spinning and preserve the status quo at least for now, he thought.

"What happens if we find an UFO?" asked Janet who was keen to know what Aaron was thinking.

"Well, that's a whole different ball game and one I've been thinking about since we decided to come out here."

"Well, what do you think?"

"We will probably find a host of local and foreign agencies plus the press all over the scene like flies on a dead carcass," replied Arron.

"So you're serious about the possibility of finding a crashed UFO or one that has landed then..?" asked Janet as she took another gulp of her beer from the food trolley.

"Remember, what you said the other day about aliens finding us first, and that their technology would be far ahead of us and their intentions could be deadly."

"Yes."

"Well, it's the same for our species. Man has conquered and invaded countries throughout history using force for its own ends. The aliens perhaps have the same agenda. We should not assume they are here to be our friends. Remember, scientists and our governments should never make assumptions, even though they do from time to time."

Aaron's mind drifted back to a time when he was invited to a government secret meeting. Back then the American government was more concerned about the future survival of humanity; yet, many there prophesied a coming financial apocalypse, which could bring an end to civilization. Even back then the government knew something they weren't sharing, but Aaron couldn't share his thoughts with Janet or anyone else, it was national security and his life and career depended on keeping silent. It had been discussed at these secret meetings even though the government were not admitting to the existence of aliens.

Aaron always thought the government or the 'deep state' as Aaron liked to refer to were not telling the truth to the public. Why would the government be so concerned with the possibility of aliens invading our planet if the risk didn't exist was his thoughts. The risk of informing the public about the existence of aliens possibly living amongst us was studied at these secret meetings and the outcomes looked grim to Aaron.

Most scientists at these secret meetings agreed the risk of informing the public about the existence of aliens was too great. Government studies had shown how many people would react to the news of aliens, so the government would keep it secret for as long as they could, he mused. Provided the aliens didn't land on the White House lawn and announce their arrival to the world the secret would be safe, Aaron said to himself. Aaron had convinced himself that certain people in the government knew a lot more about aliens and the truth. It had become obvious to Aaron over the years prior to attending those secret government meetings that the government knew the truth about aliens.

Aaron had also considered the amount of documentary evidence from around the world from credible witnesses such as airline pilots and military personnel that it wasn't easy to dismiss. As a scientist, Aaron had analysed the evidence and the logic in his mind and it would suggest their existence, and that they could have been on the planet for thousands of years.

Perhaps, aliens have been on the planet even before the evolution of man as some ancient alien theorists have contended, he mused. It was obvious to him that life and intelligent life would be a wide spread throughout the visible universe, because the universe was many billions of years older than our solar system. The logic would suggest that intelligent life could be many millions or even billions of years ahead of us. And to him, it would be no surprise to see intelligent life far different from Homo sapiens. He often thought about the paradox of man and ape. He had considered why man had superior intelligence and yet the ape with limited intelligence and nearly the same DNA had not. But, what if it was the opposite of the norm where apes had superior intelligence and man were the dumb animals, he had said himself.

Our perception, plays a major role in how we think about other animals, so we cannot be sure we are right that is the paradox, he mused. How do we know that an alien life force such as a beetle hasn't been observing us for thousands of years and can communicate intelligently in some way, he had pondered. Perhaps, the structure of Deoxyribonucleic acid (DNA) had arrived on our planet by means of an asteroid as posturized in 'Panspermia' and not by evolution on our planet. Answers to some of these enigmas often dominated his mind, as did his obsession with the threat of an asteroid hitting the earth.

His hobby in astronomy as a young boy had quickly turned into the profession he wanted to pursue at university. And it was this obsession that had led him down many avenues of research that didn't always fit with the established view.

He remembered, as a twelve year old boy sat beside his mother in the car as she drove over the via-duct and he pointed out to his mother the flames of an asteroid streaking across the sky. Possibly to land somewhere in the distance or miss the Earth by a cat's whisker, he thought. Since that day, he had an obsession with NEOs or asteroids and comets potentially hitting the Earth.

His work at the observatory often led to areas of research where he had wanted to explore further. It was at university where he first met Janet in the university library on a day like today, he thought. It was Janet that had inspired his curiosity in other topics. That day the heavens had poured and any chance of staying dry walking between lecture rooms was a non-event. The furious wind that day was virtually horizontal and blew the rain hard as if you were in a bathtub using a shower device to wash yourself. And, so it was today, the wind and rain was relentless, he said to himself.

He had considered the 'fish bowl' enigma where as far as the goldfish inside the fish bowl were concerned it was their universe. But, outside the fish bowl was a much larger universe. It was a question of scale. Our universe perhaps was like the fish bowl with another much larger universe outside, only, we don't know about it, he had pondered. Where God came into the equation, he wasn't sure, perhaps on a larger scale, he had mused.

He was always testing the 'status quo' because from just logic it would suggest that the truth never lies. He would often say to friends that one anomaly in history is often the biggest ticket in town. But, often this anomaly gets put aside because it doesn't fit the established view, and so gets forgotten about in the pages of history, yet, the truth never lies, he mused.

Then Aaron remembered, the time he had spent with Janet exploring Montana. It was when they had come across an old Cheyenne Indian mystic who told many stories about his Indian ancestors. The Indian mystic had told them stories about how the white man had destroyed much of nature without thinking first what they were doing. He had said to Aaron and Janet that they should learn to slow down. The Indian went on to explain with examples that man often creates his own disasters by not thinking first about the consequences of their actions.

The Indian mystic said that the pollution of the seas started the same time as plastics became dominate for every day materials that could be discarded. He mentioned the dumping of waste in the seas without any thought about how plastics would float away, and end up eventually eaten by animals such as whales. The pieces of plastic would eventually get stuck in the intestines of the animal and die. Man had not thought about the minuscule particles of plastic that fish would consume and how that would eventually threaten the food chain. The Indian mystic had said that when you have learnt to slow down to such an extent that you think before taking action, only then will you be with nature and not against it. The meeting with the Indian had been a spiritual experience for Janet and Aaron. The Indian had said 'less haste more speed' and these were the words that resonated in Aaron's mind.

The Indian had said to find a place where you could slow down and experience nature at its best. Aaron and Janet had found that the cliffs of the California coast were a place you could experience nature at its best. Where you could smell the sea from the breeze and where the surrounding land above the sea would turn into an orange blossom. The scent of the flowers as you relaxed and bathed in the day's sunlight was enough to send you to sleep. There were many times when they both fell asleep together, he remembered.

"What are you thinking about Aaron?" asked Janet.

"If I told you I would be breaking national security and I wouldn't want to do that," retorted Aaron with a wry smile that meant to Janet that perhaps he would if the right circumstances occurred.

"Would you like anything else?" asked the waitress with a pronounced accent. Aaron and Janet ordered another round of drinks before resuming their conversation.

"It amazing how the English language is so dominant throughout the world," said Janet while she surveyed the hotel restaurant.

"Yes, most people can say a few words or understand some simple sentences because English is a universal language and it's just as well because I can't speak a word of Mongolian," replied Aaron with laughter in his voice.

"Perhaps we should retire for the night; we have a busy day tomorrow. We have to be up early to arrange transport to the debris field," said Janet as she viewed the vista of city lights shinning in the distance from the hotel's bar's balcony.

Leaving the bar, Aaron and Janet made their way to their rooms they were both feeling the need to get some sleep. As Aaron laid there on the bed starring at the ceiling there was a knock on the bedroom door, it was Janet.

"Did you find out any news about the asteroid?" asked Aaron.

"Yes, there was an eye witness….an old goat herder. He lives in a village not far from the debris field. A village called Ayisha. I spoke to a reporter in the restaurant when you asked me to find out any information or news on the asteroid strike." replied Janet.

"Good, we will interview the goat herder tomorrow and for now I need to get some sleep. Give me a nudge in the morning. Good night, Janet."

Before Aaron fell asleep his thoughts again turned to the secret government meeting he had attended. They were probably right about the financial health of the country, he mused. Many people made ridiculous assumptions that their 401K plans would save the day, but they never really made the grade for most people in the 21 century and this was a constant worry for the future of mankind, only most people hadn't made the connection. An older population and a decreasing workforce spelt disaster, only, the general public hadn't woken up and their governments were hiding the pending disaster.

The American government hadn't made its mind up on the alternatives to the problem, but Aaron knew what one of the plans the government were seriously considering. He had been one of the delegates at the secret government 'think tank' that had met at a secret location in the state of Nevada almost two years earlier to discuss possible solutions to the problem. At the time, he had dismissed most of the recommendations as too far-fetched in his mind, but he was only one of twenty experts there with wide ranging views from the extreme to almost apathy on the problem.

The America government he considered would take the right path with the recommendations the 'think tank' had proposed, but he wasn't making the decisions it was up to unknown government officials and their agenda may have a different outcome and one he hadn't thought about. But for now, he consoled himself with the prospect of chasing UFOs as he fell asleep in the arms of Janet.

***

The following afternoon, Janet had arranged to share the charter of a helicopter with a news reporter from the New York Times. As the three of them boarded the helicopter, Janet introduced Aaron to the reporter. "Aaron, this is John Cramer, who I spoke with last night about sharing this helicopter."

"Glad to meet you and thanks for sharing the helicopter. I understand these helicopters are in short supply due to the media frenzy," said Aaron as he shook hands with John Cramer.

"Yes, they're more popular than Santa," said Cramer the reporter with a wry smile across his face.

***

Approaching the village of Ayisha, Frank Santoli and Ahmed Khan could see the village, which only consisted of a dozen homes or so with one main road that went nowhere, except into the desert. The village was totally surrounded by sand dunes and desert for miles. The helicopter touched down inside a clearing beside a stone built and corrugated roofed building. Within minutes their helicopter was surrounded by a group of children jumping and screaming with joy. Ahmed was quick to ask the children if they knew Abu Bactu the goat herder.

If by luck the children knew this man and were willing to show Frank and Ahmed where the goat herder lived. Many of the inhabitants had heard the helicopter approaching the village and had watched from their homes as Frank and Ahmed made their way down the street to the goat herder's home led by a posse of excitable children. Ahmed gave the children some money as they pointed to the home of the goat herder. The children were quick to disappear and excited at their new found wealth they now had to spend. The house was much the same as other homes in the village a mix of concrete block and stone built with a rusty corrugated steel roof. As Frank and Ahmed approached the house the door opened and Ahmed recognized the face of Abu Bactu from the TV news the day before. A well-tanned and wrinkled face with sunken eyes and a long silvery beard and with a pronounced stoop greeted Frank and Ahmed at the door.

"Are you Abu Bactu the goat herder?" asked Ahmed in the local Mongolian language.

"Yes," Abu replied in English. Abu explained that he could speak English because many different nationalities would cross these lands trading goods on their way to the 'Silk Road' and the gateway to Europe and China. They noticed he spoke with a lisp as he tried to frame his words by a lack of teeth. The old man was almost black as road tar with deep wrinkles across his face from too much sun and wind that contrasted with his long silvery beard and straggly grey thinning hair on his head.

"We are from the government. We would like to know what you saw the other day?" asked Ahmed.

"I was on the hills herding my goats when I saw an UFO, but I had been drinking, so, I'm not sure."

"When you say UFO you mean a spacecraft?" asked Ahmed.

"Yes, I have seen UFOs before."

"But, you said you had been drinking…drinking what?" asked Ahmed.

"It's called *Arkhi*, it's a milky vodka, it's very popular around here," said the old man, as Frank and Ahmed noticed, he had a wide grin on his face, which was accentuated by his lack of teeth clearly visible in his gaping cavern for a mouth.

"Okay…did you see the UFO land or crash?" asked Ahmed continuing the questioning, while Frank looked on carefully observing the goat herder.

"No. But it changed direction. So, it wasn't a meteor or asteroid," Abu replied powerfully without the effects of alcohol confusing his mind. He was confident in what he had seen. He had a sharp mind; he reminded himself that a goat herder had to be aware of everything in the mountain pastures and valleys with the ever present threat of predators willing to take from his flock given the chance. Even if he was drinking alcohol that day he still had one eye on his flock. Besides, he drank alcohol most days to keep out the cold winds that came from the north in Siberia. It was just another day for a goat herder until that UFO appeared.

"So, it was a UFO you saw?" asked Ahmed.

"Yes."

"Is there anything else you have failed to mention?" asked Ahmed.

The old man looked at Frank and Ahmed and shook his head from side to side. "No, that's it," replied Abu.

"Good, we want you not to mention to anyone that you think you saw an UFO and this money is for your silence." Abu held out his hand and Ahmed placed more money than the goat herder made in a year. "If we hear that you have broken your silence we will be back for our money," explained Ahmed. Ahmed looked at Frank and hoped for the old man's sake that there would be no need to return. Retiring the goat herder for good was not a job Ahmed welcomed but he would do it if ordered to. Orders are orders, he said to himself, especially in the CIA.

As Frank and Ahmed walked back to the helicopter, Ahmed was hoping it would be the last time and the only time he came face to face with the goat herder. "I hope you agree how I handled Abu?" asked Ahmed.

"Yes, that's why you're here, you speak the local lingo if we need it and you are always dispensable," Frank replied with a wry smile on his face. Ahmed wasn't sure if Frank meant what he had just said or he was just playing around with him. Frank didn't say another word on the matter, but he knew what he meant, it was how things were done in the CIA.

"Let's get going and find that UFO, my boss will want an update before the day is done."

***

A Space Time Apocalypse

Frank Santoli took one last look at the village before boarding the helicopter with Ahmed Khan. "Perhaps, you can tell me the rest of that story about the village named Ayisha you started last night before I fell asleep. Ahmed looked at Frank and just as the blades of the helicopter started to rotate he shook his head in disagreement. There was no way he could finish the story above the noise of the helicopter. "Perhaps, later when we get back to the hotel," replied Ahmed shouting to be heard above the ear deafening noise of the rotating helicopter blades.

It wasn't long before the helicopter was circling the same terrain as it did the day before. According to the GPS coordinates, which Frank had shown the pilot they were right above the spot the spacecraft should have landed or crashed and they couldn't see anything apart from sand dunes and rocky hills spread out for miles. Frank suggested the pilot land in a small valley not far from where they landed the day before. As Frank and Ahmed climbed a small hill to get a better view of the surrounding area they heard the familiar sound of another helicopter approaching. Frank wondered who it was. "Okay Ahmed, remember our cover story." The CIA always had a cover story and their 'Opus Finis' was to reveal as little as possible and don't offer up any information because you never know who you are really talking to. As far as any other person was concerned they were scientists on a national security project and that was all they were prepared to say.

The helicopter flew over their heads and into the next valley where it presumably landed, thought Frank. "Okay Ahmed, let's get back to business. Somewhere in that valley between those hills straight ahead is the UFO if our computer systems are correct. I have no reason to believe we are on a 'wild goose chase' because it seems other people or agencies have the same GPS coordinates that we have, so it's most likely the UFO is using stealth technology to hide its location. Do you agree?"

Ahmed thought for moment before answering. "Yes, it's all plausible. It makes sense."

"Good, somewhere in that valley is a spacecraft and it's well camouflaged. Does anything look out of place to you?"

Ahmed looked around for several minutes before answering Frank's question. Everything looked natural. The rocks and shrubs all looked in place. The valley was as large as two football fields surrounded by hills at least as high as one length of a football field with only one opening the width of a couple of family size cars. He did notice something, not quite right. "There in the distance those birds are circling something, they can't fly down. On the left before the hill becomes rockier. I think something is there."

"Ahmed, you are right. We're almost above it. I can see what you mean. If it wasn't for the birds we would never have found it."

"What do we do now Frank?" asked Ahmed with a worried look on his face almost as if he had seen a ghost. That's a good question and one I've been thinking about for some time. We don't want to get ourselves killed."

"In the meantime, let's wait and see who turns up. I reckon maybe an hour before anyone from that helicopter makes their way here. Now, would be a good time to finish your story about Ayisha and her father."

Ahmed for second was shocked, but soon realized that Frank was serious. As Frank and Ahmed sat down amongst the pebbles, rocks and large boulders that had been shaped smooth and rounded over millions of years by rivers and floods they waited. The day was getting hotter as the mid-day sun baked and reflected off the smooth and rounded rocks and pebbles on the valley floor.

"Remember, the village we saw yesterday that was named after the granddaughter of the Prophet Mohammed. It is said that a local trader who founded the village named his daughter Ayisha the same name as the granddaughter of the Prophet. The village became known as the 'village of Ayisha' and became famous for its trading and the many merchants that passed through on their way to the 'Silk Road' talked about the beauty of Ayisha. It was said that any man that laid eyes on Ayisha were then instantly mesmerized by her Arabic features. Her long hair that reached to the middle of her back shone like the color of coal. Her skin was said to be perfect in tone a mixture that complemented her dark hair. Her eyes were the color of ripened dates that gleamed and would beguile most men to their knees."

"She sounds like a real beauty…please continue Ahmed," remarked Frank, while he carefully surveyed the valley for any visitors from behind a large outcrop of boulders left behind most likely, he mused, after the last ice age.

"Okay." Ayisha's father had whittled down the potential suitors to three from an initial group of around ten. He did this by announcing that each candidate would have to bring with them a special gift for Ayisha that announced his love for Ayisha. And that each candidate not already a Muslim would have to convert to Islam before they could marry Ayisha. The special gift would be retained by Ayisha as her property even if the candidate was not chosen to marry Ayisha. One was a Christian who was called Michael; he was a local boy who tended goats and sheep for his father on the pastures between the valleys and on the mountain steppes not far from here.

"The next suitor was a devout Muslim and older than the Christian boy. His name was Memhet and worked in the metal exchange, where gold and silver were bought and sold and traded amongst the merchants of the day," said Ahmed, pausing to look at Frank as he lay on the rocks, wondering if Frank was listening to him or had he fallen asleep under the cover of his sunglasses, he mused.

"Keep going, Ahmed, I'm fully awake and interested in your story," said Frank as he adjusted his position amongst the rounded boulders trying to keep comfortable under the baking sun without falling asleep. He felt no breeze in the air to cool the hot air rising from the valley floor.

"The last candidate was a Jew. His name was Joseph, who had inherited his father's jewellery shop in a city of merchants and traders, not far from here. A place they call 'Pasha' meaning wealth."

"It's an interesting story so far, keep going," remarked Frank as he heard the sound of distant voices coming from the next valley.

"Now, the three suitors had to present a gift to Ayisha and explain why they had brought their gift."

"Michael the Christian boy presented Ayisha with 3 gold coins."

"What was the value of the gold coins?"

"I do not know?" replied Ahmed.

"Anyhow, the boy explained that the coins represented the past, present and the future. He said that the coins only held their value for that time and place. He went on to say that money and the pursuit of money regardless of other people can only lead to disaster. So, Michael then said, I present these coins as a token of my love for you, Ayisha," said Ahmed as he heard the sound of distant voices getting louder minute by minute.

"Shall I continue, Frank?" asked Ahmed.

"No. We will wait and see what these people do. You can finish the story later back at the hotel," replied Frank as he watched the people survey the valley floor. He wondered if the visitors would come across the hidden spacecraft as they had earlier that morning. It was more to do with luck and being at the right place and at the right time, he mused.

"Ah, as I predicted I can see at least three figures approaching us from the right of us. They did the same as we did the other day…they decided to take a look in the next valley as we did," said Frank.

Ahmed looked up at the approaching trio, "What do we do?"

"Nothing," responded Frank calmly before continuing, "We shall wait and see what they have to say and remember keep to our cover story."

It was nearly an hour before Aaron, Janet and the reporter had crossed the valley floor and was close enough to have a conversation with Frank and Ahmed.

"Hello, I'm Professor Aaron Mikovitz and this is my colleague Dr. Janet Taylor we're from the Near Earth Project in California. And this is John Cramer from the New York Times," said Aaron.

"Hi, my name is Frank Santoli and this is my colleague Ahmed Khan we are working on behalf of the government. We've had no luck finding the asteroid, how about you?" asked Frank.

Before Aaron could answer, Frank was busy fishing for information and was now prepared with the bait to reel them in. "We haven't found any trace of an asteroid or an UFO."

Everyone was shocked even Ahmed. "We interviewed an old goat herder who said he saw an UFO…you no… a spacecraft. But, he also said he'd been drinking that day. So, we have an unreliable eye witness and no debris."

Pausing for a moment Frank continued, "What do you think Professor?"

Aaron thought for a moment before replying, he wasn't expecting this, it court him off guard. "Perhaps, we're in the wrong area that's why we haven't found anything so far?"

"You don't believe that do you?" asked Frank incredulously.

"Well, we have no crater and no debris from a crash and no spaceship, so we have zilch. Except maybe a tan from the

A Space Time Apocalypse

burning heat of the sun. You see…this valley is protected from the Artic winds that dominate this area," responded Aaron.

Frank countered, "You seem to know a lot about this area."

"Yes." Aaron chuckled before continuing. "I've done my homework."

Janet interjected with a cute smile, "I make sure he's done his homework before he falls asleep."

Frank made a mental note of the information before suggesting where the trio should start their search. "Perhaps, you should start over there on the left of the entrance to the valley! We've been working on the right side of the valley and haven't found any evidence, so far."

Frank demonstrated with his hands that they had also found zilch. Aaron just nodded his head and turned with his companions following his general direction to the right.

Janet was the first to break the silence as she surveyed the valley floor. "What do you think of those two?"

"I haven't been thinking about them. I more concerned why we haven't found anything. All our computer systems and more can't be wrong. It landed here and perhaps we just can't see it," replied Aaron.

It sounds like a great story said the reporter, "The missing alien spacecraft."

"Well my boss will want a report and so far, we have zilch," interjected Aaron.

After about an hour of searching, Aaron caught sight of the spacecraft about 100 meters in the distance, which had suddenly appeared from its invisibility. "Look!"

"Wow."

"It's amazing, fucking amazing."

Aaron, Janet and John stood in silence and each of them in their own way admired its construction, size and presence. Aaron approximated the spacecraft to about the length of a football field, it was huge compared to any spacecraft humanity had to offer. He noticed that the spacecraft had a silvery color and was like a cucumber with a section in the middle that looked like port holes you see on an ocean liner. "I suggest you take some photos, John," said Aaron.

"You too, Janet."

Frank and Ahmed did the same with their mobile phones. "Well, so far, no one has been killed. It was a good idea to let that trio stumble on the spacecraft first," said Frank who was just as amazed as the others in the group.

"Yes, you were right, Frank," retorted Ahmed.

Frank and Ahmed stood and observed Aaron's every move as he edged closer and closer to the spacecraft. Before Aaron and his companions were no more than about 10 meters from the craft a doorway opened from the underside and a humanoid figure appeared shadowed by the sun. The figure stood at least 7 ft. from Aaron's approximation and it looked more robotic than human although it had a human form its skin resembled a lizard when it was out of the shadows.

"We mean no harm," said Shogi the lizard alien as it walked down a ramp the door opening had made to the ground.

"What do you want?" asked Aaron.

"My commander wants to speak with you and your friends aboard our spacecraft."

"They speak our language," chirped Janet quietly into Aaron's ear.

"It seems so...perhaps they've had lessons," replied Aaron rhetorically to Janet.

Aaron and his companions all felt compelled to follow even though normally they would have inclined the opposite and gone the other way. The trio followed the alien back into the spacecraft and along a corridor passing many door openings and adjacent corridors, until the alien opened another door, which slid open like the action of a camera shutter. As Frank and Ahmed stood up and revealed themselves from their hiding place they walked over to the spacecraft and also followed the trio aboard the alien's spacecraft. They too, felt compelled to follow the alien into the alien's spacecraft.

As all five of them were stood inside a room. It felt to the humans like the main control room aboard the alien's spacecraft. Aaron noticed the room had many different computer terminals placed along its walls with adjacent seats with an oval shaped control panel in the centre of the room. The terminals had different color lights flashing with what looked like some form of language text being displayed on the terminal screens. Aaron noticed the computer terminals had no accompanying key boards or input control devices like a mouse. There were large visual screens displayed on the walls of the room where each wall displayed what looked like different parts of the universe, he mused. Each screen was integrated into the wall and not a separate device like some form of conventional large TV set.

Stood by the centre control panel was another alien who wasn't that different from Shogi, thought Aaron. He noticed the head shape was slightly different more rounded and the facial features were different. No different from the human race, we are all Homo sapiens but we are unique. Even twins have differences, he mused.

"Pretty impressive," muttered Jane quietly into Aaron's ear as everyone else stood amazed at what they were experiencing.

"This is my commander Iron Smart," said Shogi. The alien commander just looked at the group of humans with its almond shaped eyes, which lit up a dark green color the moment the alien moved its head.

The two aliens looked much the same to Aaron and the group. The aliens had a shiny black metallic appearance; only, it wasn't any form of metal that the group had seen before. As the aliens moved around the room the metal moved like it had the characteristics of 'all in one' body suit like a 'wet suit' a diver would where. But the suit wasn't plastic or rubber but some form of metal compound, Aaron thought. Aaron noticed the aliens' movements were robotic at times. The aliens were similar in shape to a human, but their facial features differed radically between aliens and humans. There were no facial expressions on the aliens or facial hair or hair on their heads. But you could tell the difference between aliens by the shape of their heads and its features. The aliens' heads were like the shape of the top part of a key hole. A slender neck supporting an abnormal head, but each head had slight differences between each alien. Aaron thought, the aliens were at least eight feet tall by counting the inches that towered over him. Everything else from what Aaron could see looked normal; it had two arms and two legs. The aliens shape could be mistaken for a human at a distance on a dark night, Aaron mused.

"I hope its good news," remarked John Cramer the newspaper reporter. Everyone looked at John even the aliens who expressed no facial expression.

"We speak your language. We have been monitoring your communication channels," said Shogi the alien.

Chapter 3

"A cosmic gamma ray will hit your planet on October 23rd in less than two years' time. This will extinguish all life in its path. This type of event has happened before in the planet's history. The last time it happened 90 percent of life on this planet went extinct," said Iron Smart the alien commander.

Aaron snapped, "You are asking us to believe you…why should we?"

"You can easily check it for yourselves…look at the constellation you call Sagittarius and look for a star you have named Proximus 235pl5. That star is a cosmic gamma ray, which is travelling towards this planet you call Earth. So the light you see is getting brighter and not the other way, which means in less than two years' time the Earth and the cosmic gamma rays will collide," replied Iron Smart the alien.

"How powerful is this cosmic gamma ray?" asked John the reporter.

Aaron was first to reply, "It's the second most powerful explosion of energy after the 'Big Bang' in fact, more energy is released in that one moment than our Sun will produce in its 10 billion years of existence."

"No shit," remarked Frank.

"So why are you telling us this?" asked Janet.

"We want humanity to survive the catastrophe. That is my mission," replied Iron Smart.

"Surely, our government already knows about this coming catastrophe and hasn't informed the public," said John rhetorically.

"Maybe, but it's a huge universe and a deadly one," Aaron remarked.

Aaron remembered, the secret meetings, he had previously attended and this was one of the events covered during those meetings. The logistical problems of evacuating tens of millions of people from the countries that would be effected by the blast of high radiated particles was enormous and not least was the effects on global financial markets and public reaction. The government had conducted secret surveys on public reaction to specific events to determine how best to react to certain catastrophic events. The survey results painted a bleak outcome, where civilization just broke down as people stopped going to work and paying their mortgage excreta. As if someone had just pressed a reset button on humanity, he remembered thinking.

"I would a like meeting with your President," asked Iron Smart.

"He's not asking much?" said Janet sarcastically as she laughed. "I hope he's not too busy."

Aaron looked straight at John and asked, "Do you plan to publish this story?"

Everyone's ones attention was drawn to the reporter. John could feel their attention like cats staking their prey. This was a major story that needed to be told. Besides, it would be the editor and their bosses who ultimately made the decision to publish or not. He was just the grunt who wrote and researched the story and it wouldn't be his decision. John cursely replied, "It's not my decision; it will be up to the editor."

The 'Great Dying' about 250 million years ago is when 70 percent of land animals died and 95 percent of marine life perished. Some scientists agree that is was possibly an asteroid strike, but, many don't they argue an asteroid strike wouldn't have caused such devastation and they also cite the lack of a suitable size crater. They also cite the increased spike in life forms directly after an extinction event such as the one 250 million years ago was likely due to mutations caused by this radiation.

"This is all semantics, we have to decide what to do next," remarked Frank who was ready for a drink.

"Yes, we need to meet in the hotel bar. But, first we need to get to our helicopters and get the hell out of here before this place is invaded by a sea of reporters and asteroid hunters," remarked Aaron.

Iron Smart had given them instructions of how to make contact as soon as a meeting could be arranged with the American President. Iron Smart and their spacecraft would remain in the valley and invisible to all outsiders.

Aaron was perplexed and thinking as the group departed from the alien spacecraft. It was something Iron Smart had said about humanity. Iron Smart had said that our understanding of man's evolution was wrong, but he didn't say what was wrong. The alien robot had purposely been vague, but this plagued Aaron's mind like a bad headache that he couldn't get rid of.

As Aaron, Janet and John made their way back to their helicopter they momentarily stopped and looked back for the spacecraft, which was now invisible. Aaron remarked, "Well, there's no point in interviewing that goat herder, now, Janet."

"Yes, that's true," chirped Janet in Aaron's ear.

"What about you, John?" asked Aaron.

"No point, I have all the information I need to write the story," replied John.

As Frank and Ahmed watched the other three walk away to their helicopter they both noted the transformation of the alien's spacecraft from visible to invisible, which was instantaneously achieved in a fraction of a second. Frank had noted that it happened in a blink of an eye. But his thoughts were about national security.

Frank had a lot to consider on the helicopter flight back to the hotel. "What are your thoughts, Ahmed?"

"It's too much to take in at the moment. The whole alien thing, first confirmation of alien beings and the spacecraft, it's too much to handle. And then the coming apocalypse and where it will hit the earth and where it will be total destruction of life. And then the aliens want a meeting with our President."

Frank looked into Ahmed's eyes and calmly said, "Keep calm!"

Ahmed said, "How can I be calm, if all this is true?"

"Seriously, I have doubts about national security. Can the other three be trusted? If this gets out before we have had time to analyze the risks the whole civilized world could be plunged back to the Stone Age." Frank thinking, it could all happen in the blink of the eye, where society dislocates itself from civilization and reverts briefly back to chaos.

Frank used the time in the helicopter on the way back to the hotel to consider the options available. One option would involve retiring the other three witnesses, perhaps Ahmed as well. This option was extreme but maybe necessary to maintain national security, it would not be his decision to make, he said to himself. Another option would be to swear the other three to secrecy and to enlist them into the CIA as operatives. This option was more palatable, and to him, it made more sense. He hated retiring people, but for terrorists and alike he had no qualms. Another option would be not to do anything and just let the world know the truth. He wasn't about to make any bets in his mind about what option his boss would make. He knew the option he would take.

"What are you thinking about, Frank," asked Ahmed already alarmed at what he had seen and heard aboard the alien spacecraft.

"Our next move," replied Frank calmly.

***

Everyone had gathered in the bar of the Chinggis Khaan International Airport, hotel. Frank announced that he and Ahmed worked for the CIA and that under these circumstances asked that Aaron, Janet and John to be sworn to secrecy for the national security of America and its allies. At first, John Cramer the reporter from the New York Times was disappointed, but then agreed to be sworn in. Professor Aaron Mikovitz and Dr. Janet Taylor had no choice as they were already government employees and as such were tied to the official secrets act and this just reinforced the need for secrecy. So, they both agreed for national security reasons.

Frank announced to the group, "So, we're all agreed that what we have seen today stays secret."

Aaron stated to the group, "We need to inform the President and arrange a meeting with the President and the alien Iron Smart, immediately."

Everyone, in their own way said yes. "Perhaps, it should be Frank who can handle this?" said Janet.

"Perhaps, it should be you, Aaron?" Frank continued, "After all you are the scientist and best equipped to explain the coming cosmic rays catastrophe to the President."

"Yes, I agree Janet or myself would be best to explain the implications of the gamma ray burst, but I think, all of us need to be there with the President to convince him weren't not all insane," Aaron said calmly with a chuckle of laughter in his voice.

There was a brief moment of laughter among the group. But they all knew how serious the cataclysmic event would be for the world. One day less than two years from now the world would experience another mass extinction event.

"We will need some redundancy… In case, we become targets," said Frank.

"John, you will need to write the story of what we have seen and its implications and a means to publish should anything nasty happen to anyone of us." Frank paused before continuing, "This will be our redundancy."

"Do you really think we could become targets?" Janet fretted and continued. "I mean we're just the messengers."

"Yes, but you know what that could mean," retorted Aaron.

Frank calmly interrupted, "That's why we need the redundancy to safe guard not only our lives but the future of life on this planet. There will be interested entities that may have a different agenda. This could include stock markets and the globalization of trade continuing without the knowledge of the coming catastrophe."

"There will be some individuals in the government that will want to keep the status quo. That could include the President," remarked John.

"Yes, what would we do then?" asked Dr. Janet Taylor.

Aaron's immediate thoughts were taken back to the secret meeting in Nevada as part of his role in a secret government think tank. A delegate had proposed a major decrease in population. At the time, everyone was shocked, yet, the logic suggested otherwise. The government had plans to safeguard the diversity of seeds. So, it was not only sensible but feasible that it had plans in place to safe guard some individuals. Humanity would be saved at the cost of many billions of people. Yet, a coronal mass ejection from the Sun would be enough of a shock to civilization, he thought.

"I cannot think that far ahead," said Aaron.

Aaron continued, "We are due for a mass extinction event because we know now that it's probably happened many times in Earth's history. It happened 250 million years ago and we think it also happened 750 million years ago for sure, according to the evidence and recent technological advancements. You see up until very recently our picture of the universe was benign, but we now know the universe is a violent place." Pausing for a moment before continuing, "We may have outlived our time."

"Are we all agreed on what we must do?" asked Frank.

"Yes," was the shout from the members of the group.

"Humanity needs to know before it's too late," remarked Janet eager to let the group know how she felt.

"Tonight, Aaron and I will notify our respective bosses and in the meantime John will write the story in case we need to publish. Any future contact should be by telephone, but don't talk about anything to do with our plans. Remember, total secrecy," said Frank calmly to the group.

"I hadn't planned to be saving the world," chirped Janet quietly to Aaron in his ear.

Ahmed had been quiet for most of the discussion, but was troubled because the trajectory of the cosmic gamma ray according to Iron Smart would hit the very country he was born in. He had family that lived there. He had to tell them before it was too late. But, he would be breaking the secrecy he had sworn to obey in the CIA and within the group. "What about our families that may be affected by this gamma ray? Can we tell them?" asked Ahmed sheepishly as his face squinted with worry and wondered what the reply would be.

"For now, no," replied Frank sternly looking everyone in the eyes. "Don't worry, when the time comes to tell your families we will be in plenty of time."

"Where have I heard that?" said Janet to herself.

***

As Frank Santoli, sat on the bed in the hotel overlooking the airport, he was preparing for an early flight back to America. He had prepared his suitcase, which wasn't much just a change of clothes, underwear and toilet apparel prepared into a small carry on case of essential items for travel.

"Shall, I continue with the story about Ayisha? Frank," asked Ahmed, I think you will like the ending."

"Yes, Ahmed continue, otherwise, I'll be wondering what I have missed on the flight back home, tomorrow," replied Frank with a wry smile across his face.

Ahmed sat back on his bed in the hotel and continued with the story of Ayisha. At Frank's insistence Ahmed summarized what he had already told him before.

Ahmed explained that there were three candidates chosen. One was a Jew, one was a Christian and one was a Muslim. Each of them brought a gift for Ayisha.

"You remember, Frank…Michael the Christian brought three gold coins," said Ahmed.

"Yes, I remember."

"Michael, are you willing to convert to Islam?" asked Ayisha's father who was surprised by the quickness of his reply.

"Yes, I am willing to convert to Islam to marry your daughter," replied Michael eyeing the prize of marring Ayisha worth the conversion from Christianity to Islam.

"The Jew presented Ayisha with a white pearl necklace. The Jew had said that the pearls had been gathered from the pearl clams from the South China Sea. The Jew explained that the necklace consisted of 365 individual pearls and represented the number of days in a year and how much each day of love he would cherish married to Ayisha," said Ahmed as he continued with the story, which had now stretched over the past couple of days. He wondered if Frank was getting tired of the story that had been stopped and started over the past few days. But, he knew Frank would appreciate the ending and reveal the choice Ayisha would make with the help of her father.

"Joseph, are you willing to convert to Islam?" asked Ayisha's father who was again surprised by the quickness of the Jew's reply.

"Yes, I am willing to convert to Islam to marry your daughter," replied Joseph as he also began eyeing the prize of marring Ayisha that was worth the conversion from Judaism to Islam.

"The Muslim called Memhet presented Ayisha with a beautiful black stallion. The horse was a thoroughbred Arabian stallion. The stallion had been bred for speed and stamina. The coat of the stallion shone like the twinkle of sun light upon a calm sea. This Arabian stallion would need special feed not like the shaggy work horses that graze the Mongolian steppe, which were the type of horses so favoured by Genghis Khan. These horses enabled Genghis Khan to conquer a vast land mass from Eastern Europe to the land of China. All because this type of horse could graze on its natural surroundings rather than the need for special feed, which would be needed for an Arabian thoroughbred stallion," said Ahmed as he looked at Frank stretched out on the hotel bed.

"What happened next, Ahmed?" asked Frank.

"Be patient, Frank. I'm nearly finished," replied Ahmed.

"I can't wait for the *coup d'etat*. If there is one?" asked Frank

"Memhet, you are already a follower of Islam. So, I will ask you why you follow Islam and not Christianity or Judaism?" asked Ayisha's father.

"Because, I was taught from an early age by my parents who are devout Muslims," replied Memhet.

"Yes, but you are a man and now have the choice to follow any religion should you so wish. So, what is it about Islam that holds you in its grip," asked Ayisha's father.

"It is the poetry of love throughout the Quran that I seek to live my life by and hopefully be married to Ayisha," replied Memhet.

"Thank you Memhet, Joseph and Michael for your gifts. It's now time to ask you to leave the room for a short time, while Ayisha and I discuss who has won the right to marry my daughter."

Ahmed explained that it was now the time to pick who would marry Ayisha. Ayisha would have the final say on who she would like to marry. Ayisha's father was only there in an advisory role. Ahmed then explained that it would be the wishes of Ayisha that would sway the day and even though she trusted her father's opinion she didn't always agree with him.

Meanwhile, as Ayisha and her father discussed each candidate in a separate room attached to the main hall the candidates waited anxiously for news that they were the one that would marry the beautiful Ayisha.

"You have to understand, Frank, most, if not all marriages, at these times were arranged marriages. The difference about this marriage was the ending and one little word that perhaps you have missed like most people do?" explained Ahmed with a wry grin that crossed his face and from cheek to cheek.

Eventually, after about an hour, Ayisha and her father emerged from the room and both had pleasant smiles to show the candidates.

"First, I would like to thank all the candidates for their patience and honesty throughout this process. I would like to announce that Ayisha has chosen Michael and that they will be married as soon as preparations can be made. Ayisha, would like to say a few words before you leave," said Ayisha's father.

"We made a list of demands at the beginning of this process so that a manageable number of suitable candidates could be found. We made no demands on the value of the gift to me nor made any stock in their value. So it's my pleasure that the gifts from Joseph and Memhet be returned or be donated to the poor, it's your choice. Finally, thanks for making it a difficult choice," said Ayisha.

Ahmed explained that friends and family that had witnessed the process clapped hands as Ayisha and Michael walked into the courtyard adjacent to the house, which also served as a storehouse for much of what Ayisha's father traded. Fresh flowers on the Juniper trees scented the air. The fragrance from the Juniper trees would linger long after the celebrations had ended, long into the night.

Ahmed said that Ayisha and Michael connected like a pair of swans who mate for life. Their bond of love shone like their marriage would be made in heaven. Ahmed explained that they looked into each other's eyes with love and then they gently kissed each other.

"Holding each other tightly, Ayisha said, "Do you want to know how I made my decision?"

"No. I don't want to know," replied Michael. "Does it matter?"

"Yes. I do want to know," again Michael replying with an alternative scenario. "And it does matter."

"Well, my father asked each candidate three questions asking for a specific answer. There would be one question of the three questions designed to show which were listening. The answer proved which candidates were listening and which were not. It turns out that two of the candidates were not listening," said Ayisha

Ahmed explained that each candidate was asked three questions and each answer recorded by Ayisha's father. Ahmed said that three was a sacred number in Islam as well as Christianity and Judaism. The choice of three candidates and three questions was considered by Ayisha's father to be an auspicious test to find the ideal choice for Ayisha to marry. Ahmed explained that Ayisha's father had said that the test would prove which candidate to pick.

The three questions that were asked are as follows," said Ahmed.

"Why do you want to marry Ayisha?"
"Why did you pick the gift you brought, today?"
"Why do your practice your religion?"

Do you remember what each candidate gave as an answer?" asked Ahmed.

"Not completely, don't forget you have been telling this story over several days," replied Frank.

"I will remind you of their answers," said Ahmed.

Ahmed first listed the answers that Michael had given. He then listed the answers that Joseph had given. Finally, Ahmed listed the answers that Memhet had given.

"We already know who Ayisha picked to marry," said Frank who was rhetorically answering Ahmed.

"Yes, you are right, Frank. But, did you spot the two who were not listening?" asked Ahmed.

"No, I didn't before I knew the answer."

"Did you spot the two that were not listening?" asked Ahmed again with a wry smile that curled across his lips.

"I will write out my two questions. And we will see who is right or not," announced Ahmed.

Ahmed wrote out the two questions and the two answers that were given and waited for Frank to do the same. Ahmed felt like he had won the day.

"Okay, sounds like a plan. I will apply some maths theory and my memory and I should be able to tell you," retorted Frank who was happy to play Ahmed's game before he felt the pangs of sleep would curtail their game.

Ahmed and Frank looked at each other's answers and they were both the same. Ahmed was amazed that Frank had come up with basically the same answers as his.

"How did you do it?" asked Ahmed who was curious to know the answer. He was like a child waiting for Christmas day to arrive.

"I will tell you in the morning," replied Frank as he started to fall asleep comfortable in the knowledge that Ahmed could wait for the answer. After all he had waited several days for the story to finish, it was now his turn to wait. Frank fell asleep with a slight grin across his face.

***

"Hello, this is Frank Santoli. I have my report for you, sir."

Michael Stubbs a section chief in the CIA had been patiently waiting for Santoli's report, but was over roared by what Frank had to report on the phone.

"The asteroid turned out to be an alien spacecraft on a mission to warn humanity of an impending cataclysm. Approximately two years from today a cosmic gamma ray will obliterate all life. Around half of the Earth will be affected. And the alien commander called Iron Smart wants a meeting with the President."

Frank continued, "I was present with four other people on the spacecraft when we were informed of the impending doom. This included Professor Aaron Mikovitz and Dr. Janet Taylor both from the South California Observatory. A reporter from the New York Times called John Cramer. Also Ahmed Khan our CIA operative in Mongolia was present.

Frank briefly wondered what his boss was thinking as he relayed his report over the phone.

"Why haven't we picked up this cosmic gamma ray before?" queried Stubbs.

"Professor Aaron Mikovitz is looking into this and checking the accuracy of what the alien told us. I should hear from the professor some time, tomorrow," retorted Frank.

"If it wasn't you, Frank…then I wouldn't believe a word. Well, you better get back to DC and give me a full written report."

"Okay, but what about arranging a meeting with the President?" asked Frank.

"That can wait until we have read the report and analyzed the information," snapped Stubbs.

In that minute as the phone went dead, Frank had his doubts about his boss's sincerity. He couldn't put his finger on it, but something wasn't quite right. It was something Stubbs had said before leaving for Mongolia, recalled Frank.

As Frank settled down in his seat aboard the Lear Jet, he started to think what it was that his boss had said before leaving the States. For most of the journey back it played on his mind. He went over it again and again what his boss had said about the mission. It would come to him eventually, he said to himself. In the meantime, he thought about the story Ahmed had told him about the girl Aisha and fell asleep.

***

As Professor Aaron Mikovitz and Dr. Janet Taylor arrived back in California from Mongolia they both felt the urgency to get back to the observatory. On the long drive back to the observatory from the airport they discussed what the alien had said about the coming catastrophe.

"I can't believe this is happening," said Janet starring into Aaron eyes as he watched the dusty road ahead for stray animals that he often encountered on his daily drive up the mountain to the observatory.

"Yes. I feel the same, but it's going to happen according to the alien in less than two years' time," replied Aaron trying to keep his eyes on the road ahead and not let his mind amble about what the alien had said.

"What are we going to do?" asked Janet trying to continue the conversation and rationalize her thoughts.

There was a few minutes before Aaron answered, his mind was thinking about what Iron Smart the alien robot had said about man's evolution. "We are to follow the plan we discussed with the others in the group at the hotel in Mongolia. We have no choice, but to follow the plan," replied Aaron aware of the stress in Janet's voice, while he tried to stay focused driving the car to the observatory.

"I just hope we make it."

"Do you remember what Iron Smart said about the evolution of man?" asked Aaron.

"I don't think that's important right now, Aaron," replied Janet with anger at Aaron for thinking about something the alien had said about man's evolution. "What's so important about man's evolution when the world is about to experience a mass extinction not seen since the Permian extinction?"

"That's just it. Why mention it at all? I mean…Iron Smart said it for a reason. There must be more to it that I need to find out," replied Aaron.

"Do you really think it's that important, Aaron?"

"Yes. I really do. Remember what Iron Smart said. He said our history of man's evolution was wrong. There has to be more…and I intend to find out and figure out the clues. It could be more important than we think. Who would you suggest I talk to about the evolution of man?"

"Do you remember Dr. Helen Baring? It was at that party we attended last year for Joe's birthday when I introduced you to Helen and we briefly spoke about one of her theories on evolution, do you remember?" replied Janet who was now beginning to calm down after the stress of the past few days. She was glad to be thinking about something else. Inside her mind, she had begun to forget the last few days.

"Yes. I do remember. Do you have her contact details? I would like to contact her and make an appointment to visit her as soon as possible," replied Aaron while noticing that Janet's voice had become calm and more lucid, rather than the tears and stress seen previously on her face.

As Aaron pulled into the carpark outside the observatory he noticed his boss's car. He couldn't help thinking about what his boss would say and how he would explain it. After all he thought how often do you meet an alien robot and get a chance to save many lives. He glanced over at Janet and said, "I hope the boss believes us, otherwise, he will think we have gone crazy from too much sun out in the Gobi desert."

"Sometimes I think this is crazy. We went to the Gobi searching for a meteor crash and found aliens and the knowledge that the world is about to experience a mass extinction not seen for hundreds of millions of years."

"Yes, I know…but we have to think about the many millions of lives we can save," replied Aaron.

"Yes. You are right, but it still sounds crazy," retorted Janet.

"Crazy or not, we and the other members of the group have a duty to save as much of humanity and lives as possible."

"Well, I hope Malcolm is in a good mood, otherwise, he could just fire us on the spot," replied Janet in a jovial tonal voice in her manner.

"That reminds me…dig out those contact details on that anthropologist as soon as you get a chance," retorted Aaron.

As Aaron and Janet walked into their boss's office and began their verbal report of their trip to Mongolia. Aaron's first words were, "I hope you can keep a secret? Otherwise, your life and mine and Janet's will be in danger from what we about to tell you."

The middle aged coloured man sat behind his desk raised his spectacles upon his almost bald head and for first time in many years looked intrigued. He gently caressed his moustache. His belly was a dominant feature that showed he needed more exercise and less time spent behind a desk managing a group of scientists and technicians.

"Yes. Of course I can keep a secret," replied Malcolm Spencer the chief operating executive of the South California Observatory. He had kept many secrets to himself as part of a government agency think tank that reported to the President of United States on matters of national security.

A Space Time Apocalypse

***

Professor Aaron Mikovitz and Dr. Janet Taylor wasted no time informing their boss of the catastrophe awaiting much of life on Earth. Even though Aaron and Janet had made a pledge with Frank Santoli and the others in the group to keep silent about what Iron Smart the alien had told them. It was understood within the group that certain people would have to be informed. Aaron's and Janet's boss was to be informed because he had channels of communication to the America President. If Frank Santoli failed in his efforts to secure a meeting with the President then they would use the lines of communication that Aaron's and Janet's boss possessed. It would be a risk, but Aaron and Janet had said that keeping a secret this big from their boss would be virtually impossible given what Frank Santoli had tasked them to do. The more people you inform said Frank the less likely the secret remains a secret.

Frank Santoli and the others in the group also knew the benefits of redundancy. If one failed then the other had a chance of securing a meeting with the President. Frank had been demonstrative in the need for redundancy and the need for secrecy; the two being mutually exclusive were Frank's words. The task for the group was now a disjoint and redundancy would play a part in safeguarding their lives and hopefully the lives of millions of people.

"And the alien called Iron Smart wants a meeting with the President of United States," said Aaron.

"This is a fantastic story and one that may take some time to digest," said Malcolm Spencer chief operating executive of the South California Observatory.

"Why haven't we picked up this cosmic gamma ray before?"

"It's a big universe and one where mistakes in analyzing data can happen. But, nonetheless, we are checking the data as we speak," retorted Aaron.

Janet interrupting said, "Somewhere out there is our answer."

"What about the meeting with the President? If this is true then we have to see the President and arrange a meeting with the alien?" queried Aaron. He knew something wasn't right the minute the alien had said WR104. The star WR104 was a little known star system in the constellation of Sagittarius. Was this a deep state conspiracy, he wondered.

"We have been sworn to secrecy and so you must be…you can't inform family or friends for now," continued Aaron explaining the implications of mass panic and the risk to the group's lives, including Spencer's life.

Aaron thought the government needed to create an 'Ark' of some kind to save the diversity of species as well as millions of people. "There is much the government can do and should and we only have less than two years to do it," stated Aaron.

"Iron Smart said that he had been here twenty years before and had passed on the same message to humanity. Why total silence on the part of the government? It doesn't make sense," remarked Aaron.

"Let's see what the data shows," said Spencer. "Before, we get too far ahead of ourselves."

Janet rhetorically chirped, "Easier said than done."

They both looked at Janet as she continued with her views. "It's all about the angle of augmentation. If that cosmic ray is pointing in our direction then all we can do is get out of the way. We may go back hundred years or several thousand…it all depends how we handle the blast."

"Have we ever handled world events as a responsible species?" retorted Aaron.

"Yes," said Spencer. "But, it's usually when it's too late."

As the trio stood in thought Aaron's mobile phone rang, it was Jamie Okeke their PHD student who did much of the collating of data for the scientists based at the observatory. Jamie was an African American born in Los Angeles, California who won a scholarship to attend UCLA to study art. After realizing, his talents lie elsewhere he gained a degree in computer science. Jamie was often referred to as the 'lab rat' because of his abilities to see and find the most obscure data.

"WR104 is heading straight for us like standing straight down the barrel of a gun. But, there's more….you have to see this," Jamie said to Aaron with urgency in his voice.

"Okay, see you in a minute," replied Aaron as he finished the mobile phone conversation with Jamie.

"That was confirmation of the information given to us by the alien Iron Smart, so what are you going to do now, Spencer?"

There was a long silence before Spencer broke the tense moment. Before you reply Spencer let me see what Jamie has found. "I will be back in a few minutes for your response," replied Aaron.

It was a quick walk along the corridor to the main computer control room for Aaron and Janet. Both of them were intrigued about the information Jamie the 'lab rat' had found. Sat amongst an array of computer terminals Jamie was busy hacking away, which is what he did best. His scruffy appearance hid his brilliance at finding information where no one else had the skills. Clad in jeans and a surf t-shirt he looked more like he was on holiday then working for a living. His long brown dreadlock hair was often confused by onlookers. Jamie was often mistakenly taken for a girl because of his hair. Besides, all this difference, the management of the observatory realized early on that Jamie was an asset to his colleagues.

"What have you found out, Jamie?" asked Aaron.

"It would seem that star formation you gave me is a 'ghost' word," replied Jamie.

"Explain what you mean…a ghost word. Is that what you said?" asked Janet.

"Yes. Someone or some organization has taken steps to make that star formation a 'ghost' word," replied Jamie.

Jamie explained that from that moment forward the word would become a 'ghost' word, and would be essentially classified and easily removed from all internet servers by means of a robot called a 'bot' algorithm that searched and removed all data linked to that word.

"I have tried to search for 'WR104' on the government web and the Internet, but all I get is 'classified' on our systems and no significant information on the Internet," stated Jamie.

"This is significant and what we now know to be true." said Aaron.

"Those bastards have known all along," said Janet angry at the betrayal of the trust and country she had grown up in and believed in.

"Am I missing something here?" asked Jamie confused at Janet's and Aaron's reaction to the news he had given them.

"Only the biggest story ever!" remarked Aaron.

"WR104 is about to hit Earth in less than two years and wipe out a large portion of life unless we do something, now!" continued Aaron. "The Earth is about to be hit by cosmic gamma rays that will destroy all living things in the hot zone."

"From Africa to the Artic we have to save as much as we can."

"What a can of worms for these countries," stated Janet quietly to Aaron and Jamie.

"Afterwards they will cease to exist. Any country in the hot zone will no longer exist as a country, but we can save their fauna, flora and people.

"I guess, you should tell me what's going on?" asked Jamie.

"Janet and I with three other people met with an alien aboard their spacecraft and they told us about the impending doom affecting Earth. And we have now confirmed the information is correct. The angle of augmentation of the supernova is aimed straight at us. We are looking down the barrel of a gun and it's already been fired. We have less than two years to save life," remarked Aaron.

"Yes, that's if this is not a conspiracy…because I can smell a rat in all this. Now, we have to find out who the rats are," stated Aaron.

Aaron then explained to Jamie the limits of the hot zone and what could stand a chance of survival providing you were standing in the right place on the edges of the hot zone.

On the outer edges of the hot zone due to the curvature of the earth life would probably stand a better chance of surviving the blast of highly radiated particles because the particles will have to travel through more of the earth's atmosphere before they hit the earth's crust. Aaron went on to explain that highly radiated particles called 'neutrino particles' are invisible to us and will radiate enough radiation to kill all life within seconds to days of exposure. These particles will go through mountains as if they weren't there, he explained.

"Shit, we don't stand a chance, unless, we are on the other side of the world," remarked Jamie.

"You could call them the ghost particles," stated Aaron.

"Forget about concrete bunkers or the substation that's for sure," chirped Janet who wasn't sure of anything working in the future if circumstances was to prevail.

"Before, we can go any further raise your right hand!" announced Aaron pausing to make sure Jamie was listening to him before continuing.

"First, you have to swear to secrecy for the national security of America. Are you willing to do that?" asked Aaron.

Aaron had considered the options on whether to tell Jamie the truth. He surmised that Jamie would find out the truth either from one of the group or his dedication to researching the data. He was probably already a 'person of interest' somewhere on a database and he could already be endangered. So, it made sense in Aaron's mind to tell Jamie the truth before Jamie started blogging to his friends and before long the truth would have spread to all corners of the planet.

"Yes, of course. I swear to secrecy," replied Jamie. Now, tell me what the hell is going on?"

"In less than two years' time a cosmic gamma ray from WR104 supernova is about to destroy at least fifty percent of the planet. It's heading straight for Earth and nothing can stop it.

"Why haven't we heard about this supernova...WR104 before?" asked Jamie.

"Yes, how could the scientific community miss such an event?" asked Janet.

Aaron looked at Jamie and Janet and they were as puzzled as he was. "I don't know?" replied Aaron.

"One thing for sure...the government has its hands in this," declared Jamie.

Since the first cyber-attacks during the early twenty first century governments namely America has sought ways of protecting their computer networks and systems. Government agencies such as the CIA, NSA and others were protecting Americans from hostile cyber warfare perpetrated by rogue nations as well as criminal gangs and individuals. Being able to cross reference separate databases to build profiles of individuals is essential in the war against terrorism. Using flags to process data is just a process of data mining where certain words can be isolated and flagged and manipulated by those in control of the algorithmic bots surfing the internet. It would be very easy for a government to censor or indeed control access to that data, purely by means of intelligent use of artificial intelligence controlling the bots used to troll the Internet. A seek and destroy bot could be used to remove data from servers without causing any attention from the general public.

Over time the knowledge associated with a certain word would disappear and any information that is available is what they the government's allows you to read. Your data has become redacted without you the reader being aware of it. That's how simple it was for governments to control the people since the dawn of the digital age.

"The government could easily do this…to WR104," continued Aaron. "Jamie, download all the information you can find on the web and the Internet. We need to find out as much as possible."

"What do you think, Janet?" asked Aaron.

"We will be alerting those that have been guarding this secret," remarked Janet with a tone of voice that betrayed how afraid she was of the possible consequences.

Aaron could see the grip of fear across the face of Janet as he tried to look for answers, but inside he also felt the chill of fear creep across his body. He knew he had no choice; he had to go on for humanity.

""We have no choice, Janet. We have to inform the President. And hopefully the rest of the world," declared Aaron.

***

"I've got those contact details you wanted for the anthropologist," retorted Janet as she checked her email and contacts on her computer terminal.

"Let me dial that number and make an appointment with the good doctor. There is no time to waste," said Aaron.

"Hello is that Dr. Helen Baring."

"Yes," answered Dr. Helen Baring.

"We met last year at Joe's fortieth birthday party. I was introduced to you by Dr. Janet Taylor. My name is Professor Aaron Mikovitz. I'm the leading astronomer and scientist at South California Observatory. I understand from Dr. Janet Taylor that you have an interesting theory about the evolution of man and I would like to come and see you as soon as possible."

"Yes. Of course I remember you. I'm the head of the anthropology department here at Berkeley. If you can make it here tomorrow at around 2pm then we will discuss what you want to know. Will Janet be accompanying you?" asked Dr. Helen Baring.

"No, she is busy here at the observatory," replied Aaron.

"That's a shame…it would have been good to catch up on old times. Did Helen mention that we went to the same university and became friends and that we often dated the same boys? Not at the same time, of course, but it was like that at UCLA."

"No, she never mentioned how you became friends," replied Aaron.

"Can I ask why you need to see me in such a hurry? Perhaps, I can prepare some notes for you?" asked Helen in a matter of fact way. She was intrigued as to why the professor was in such a hurry and willing to spend the time and money to come to see her.

"I was given some information about the evolution of man a few days ago and I would like to hear what you have to say on the matter. See you tomorrow when I have many questions to ask. And thanks for letting me come and see you so quick after just one phone call," retorted Aaron not willing to say too much on the phone just in case the government were already listening to his calls. He already knew that the relevant government agency could back track all digital communications and it would be wise not to say too much on the phone.

"See you tomorrow and goodbye for now," answered Dr. Helen Baring.

***

"Okay, Janet, let's see what Spencer has to say," said Aaron.

As Aaron and Janet walked the short distance along the corridor to Malcolm Spencer's office they both wondered what their boss would have to say, now that they had the facts about the supernova.

"Jamie, has confirmed the angel of augmentation and we are looking down a barrel of a gun. And there is more. Jamie says the supernova is a 'ghost' word, meaning that someone or some organization has been actively removing all references to its existence on the Internet and government web servers," said Aaron.

"What do you want me to do?" asked Malcolm Spencer who was used to giving orders not the other way round.

"Do nothing for now," replied Aaron.

"Yes, don't tell anyone about what you now know," interjected Janet with a commanding tone of voice.

"Let's wait and see if Frank Santoli the CIA agent can get to the President before we make a move. Is that understood?" asked Aaron who also spoke in a commanding tone of voice.

"Your life as well as our lives depends on you keeping quiet, until, we need your connections with the government," interjected Janet who had found a new mojo. And she enjoyed telling her boss what to do under the circumstances for a change.

"We swore you to secrecy, so we expect that you uphold your end of the equation. Otherwise, we could all end up pushing up daises," said Aaron pausing a minute and looking directly into Spencer's brown eyes before continuing. "Don't make the mistake of using your computer to find out any information on this supernova. They will be watching or a bot algorithm will know that you have been searching for this information. And don't tell any friends or family until, we think it's safe to do so. Is that clear?" asked Aaron.

"Yes, I understand. But you make this sound menacing," replied Spencer who felt the sweat from his brow slowly roll down one side of his face.

"It is deadly serious," interjected Janet who wanted to get her penny worth with a cold tone of voice aimed directly at her boss.

"In the meantime, I have Jamie searching the Internet and our web servers to see if he can find out any more information. He is already a target of interest, so we don't need more people risking their lives. Whatever information that Jamie finds we will pass on to you to read. But, don't keep any of this information on your computer or in a paper file, just in case the government comes looking for it. Make sure you destroy it by burning it. We will need you as our redundancy should we require it at a later date. The CIA agent Frank Santoli talked a lot about the need for redundancy. When the time comes it may be you who gets to the President and saves the world," said Aaron.

"What do you want me to do, now?" asked Spencer.

"Quite, frankly nothing just sit…your fat ass on it," interjected Janet who hadn't felt embolden until the last few days.

"Okay, let's keep it civil, Janet," interjected Aaron who watched as Janet had become more and more emboldened over the last few days. He was aware that her feelings had been hurt badly since the alien had given them the bad news. It had wrecked her plans for marriage possibly, he mused.

"There is no need to talk like that, Janet. I'm still your boss," said Spencer who felt his authority disappear overnight.

"Okay, let's all calm down. We have a lot to do and we all need to work together. Remember, we are working to save as much of life as we can. It's our responsibility to act like adults," said Aaron as he looked at Janet and Malcolm for a positive reaction.

"Sorry, Malcolm, I get carried away sometimes. I don't know, but since the alien visit I haven't felt the same," said Janet with a calm tone of voice willing to apologise for the outburst at Malcolm even though it cut against the grain of her character.

"I accept and I am overweight," said Malcolm Spencer with a chuckle of laughter in the tone of his voice.

***

"Hello, is that you, Frank? It's Aaron here." Aaron was quick to phone Frank Santoli with the information about the supernova he had been waiting for.

"Everything the alien told us is true. We're looking down the barrel and we can't avoid it. We're doing some more data crunching to confirm the date the cosmic gamma ray burst will hit the Earth.

"Okay, is there anything else?" asked Frank.

"Yes, it looks like a conspiracy. All relevant information concerning WR104 has been suppressed by the government," replied Aaron.

"Well, we knew something was up," remarked Frank in a jovial tone of voice.

"Oh, I've had to tell our data analyzer, Jamie. It was the lesser of two evils. He was bound to blog to his friends around the world and before long the Internet would be live with all kinds of stories. Anyway, I have sworn him to secrecy," stated Aaron in a manner of fact way hoping Frank would see the sense in what he had done so far.

"For now you did the right thing, Aaron. We knew the story was huge and could break at any time," remarked Frank.

Frank continued, "Okay, let me know of any other developments and I will inform you if there is any movement my end."

The phone went dead and Aaron started thinking of what was his next step before the world should know. And Frank was thinking the same; he had to inform his boss to confirm the bad news. It would be his boss's decision to move the information up the chain of command and ultimately to the President of the United States.

In the meantime, Frank had asked Ahmed Khan to make further enquiries about WR104 with the task of finding evidence to support the alien's claim they brought the message to Earth some twenty years earlier.

Chapter 4

The short flight to Berkeley to see Dr. Helen Baring was uneventful for Aaron. He had made some notes on the plane on what the alien Iron Smart had said. He knew he had to be careful and not let the cat out of the bag. Besides, he mused that the evolution of man was a subject the good doctor would be enthusiastic about discussing. He was not likely to fall into a trap and start discussing the coming apocalypse. It would be safer that the good doctor was kept in the dark and safer for both of them, he thought. The taxi ride from the airport to the university brought back memories of the times he spent dating Janet and the wild parties they both attended. There was good chance that Dr. Helen Baring also attended some of the same wild student parties, but he could not remember her face.

As the taxi pulled into the main carpark of the university, he paid the driver and thanked him. The taxi driver had told him a story that had lifted his spirits about the goodness of some of humanity on the journey to the university. He had decided to walk across the campus to the science building where the anthropology department was situated on the second floor overlooking much of the university grounds. Helen had given him clear directions, which made the task of finding the anthropology department a breeze, he thought.

As he made his way into the science building, he felt like a student again as he watched students pouring out of a lecture room like an unstoppable flood of water going in one direction. He did feel like a student wanting to learn what the alien Iron Smart was suggesting. His mind briefly turned a few pages back to what the alien had said. The alien had said man's evolution is not what you currently believe. But, there was something else. The alien had given him a clue. It was now up to him to search out the truth, whatever that could be, he surmised as he read the text on the door to the anthropology department. There were several members of the faculty listed on the door as well as Dr. Helen Baring located in room 289. Aaron walked down the corridor to room 289 and opened the door and entered to an office divided in two. He remembered what Helen had said about her secretary being efficient, but not always accommodating. What she meant by that

Aaron was not sure and he had no time for small talk on the phone. Aaron had decided not to press the doctor on the matter.

"Hello, can I help you," said the secretary in a warm considerate manner.

"Hi, I am Professor Aaron Mikovitz. I have an appointment with Dr. Helen Baring at 2pm."

"Yes, Dr. Baring told me you were coming. She didn't mention how good looking you are."

"She doesn't really know me," replied Aaron blushing at the compliment he had not expected considering how perhaps the doctor considered her secretary. But perhaps she had other reasons, he was not privileged too, he thought. Women just like men are often in competition for the opposite sex in a working and social environments. The rivalry between sexes often leads to jealousy, he mused.

This was part of man's evolution according to Darwin where inherited traits that help a species survive and are then passed on from one generation to the next, he mused.

As Aaron followed the secretary into Dr. Helen Baring's office his first impression was the amount of general clutter that engulfed the room. Piles of folders and papers were stacked on every available flat surface from the floor and on the large brown old mahogany desk the doctor sat behind.

"Hello, Professor Aaron Mikovitz. I have been looking forward to our meeting. Please take a seat!"

"Thank you and thanks again for seeing me so soon."

"Now, how can I help?" asked Dr. Helen Baring as she removed her spectacles and smiled directly into Aaron's eyes before blushing and flicking her long jet black hair that caressed her shoulders like a model preparing to be photographed. Her eyes were deep brown and her olive skin reminded Aaron of the girls he would see on his visits to the Holy Land. The Arabic and Jewish genetics were at play here, he surmised.

"I understand from Dr. Janet Taylor that you have a theory on the evolution of man that differs from the mainstream view," replied Aaron as he caught a cute smile curl across the doctor's face.

"I don't know what Janet has told you…so I shall start at the beginning. Is that alright with you? We have plenty of time," stated Dr. Helen Baring.

"Yes. Please continue."

"You, no doubt, have heard about Darwin's general theory of evolution and the evolution of man?" Helen hesitated momentarily as she stared at Aaron for his facial reaction, wondering if Aaron had the patience to sit and listen from the beginning. "In Darwin's book the 'Origins of Species' he puts forward a theory that he called Natural Selection, which is the mainstream theory. Darwin also suggested that all living organisms originate from a single cell on what he called the tree of life. Every living organism according to Darwin could be traced back to this single cell. Now, this is a theory and not fully proven, although it does sound plausible. After all this is the established view and what is taught in schools and colleges around the world. Darwin viewed this tree upside down to a single stem and the branches of the tree would represent the different types and species. Now, over time…many millions of years a species would evolve, but with common ancestors because of the branches represented on the tree of life. Because of the way we inherit traits and characteristics we often refer this to so-called genes, and by the way there is no such thing as genes. The word 'gene' was coined by biologists to try to describe and quantify inherited characteristics. That was the belief for many years, but we now know there is no such thing as genes. But for now, we will continue using the term genes for the sake of simplicity. Those genes with characteristics beneficial to the organism through Darwin's theory of Natural Selection would progress through each generation. Each generation would pass on its DNA to the next generation and so on. So, over a considerable amount of time many millions of years a new species would evolve on a different branch of the tree of life, but, with a common ancestor. Please be patient with me. I have summarized pages and pages of theory into a few sentences, so I hope you are following the essence so far of Darwin's theory?" said Helen waiting for Aaron to acknowledge he understood what so far she had said.

"Please, continue…Helen. I'm enjoying myself," said Aaron with a wry smile on his face. He was also wondering when Helen was going to reveal her theory. He was already willing to accept what Helen had to say about the concept of genes.

"Now, listen carefully this is where it gets interesting," she said raising the tone of her voice to Aaron much like a teacher does to a classroom full of noisy students to get their attention. "Darwin decided to publish his theory of 'Natural Selection' after many years of research, but also after many years of deliberation, because he had major doubts about his conclusions. He was almost cajoled into publishing at the time by a friend and the publisher because another naturalist Alfred Wallace was about to publish his theory that was essentially the same as Darwin's theory of evolution."

"What was the problem?" asked Aaron as Helen paused to catch her breath. Aaron was intrigued to know the reasons why Darwin was unsure about his theory of Natural Selection.

Helen said smiling, "Because Darwin's proposal on the origin of species by Natural Selection had many holes. More holes than the holes on a golf course. Darwin was unsure and the major problem about the origin of species was Natural Selection. Because he couldn't quite square through his theory of Natural Selection…how we…that is, how humans developed intelligence. We have what we could call 'super intelligence' not seen in other animals or organisms as far as we know.

Helen pausing for a minute while she caught her stride and looked into Aaron's eyes before continuing. "There are other issues as well that I will get to later. Aaron, can you understand the problems that Darwin faced and why he was initially reluctant to publish his book?"

"Yes, but it's not how we were taught at school," remarked Aaron.

Helen agreed by nodding her head before continuing, "Yes, that is the trouble with science and knowledge. We often find out many years after an accepted concept or theory that has been taught as the truth turns out not to be the case. I will explain some of these so-called truths as I continue with my lecture. It is a lecture because this is how I explain my theory on the evolution of man to other people willing to listen. Whatever, I say is based on facts and logic as you will see."

"Sorry, but what is your theory?" asked Aaron slightly irritated at Helen's remarks.

Helen said shrugging her shoulders, "It beats me…Aaron, how some people can't wait because they lack patience. But, let me finish. I haven't told you my theory yet."

"Okay. Continue Helen. Never mind me, you know I lack the patience of a Saint," replied Aaron smiling at his cute remark to the doctor.

"You are right, Aaron. Every schoolchild is taught the same throughout the world. Darwin's theory of Natural Selection has never been seriously challenged because the main stream establishment of science considers it to be a sound theory. And, every time a scientist puts forward a flaw in Darwin's theory the establishment come up with a plausible reason to argue against this," said Helen eagerly watching Aaron's reactions as she laid the groundwork before revealing her theory.

"Before I layout my theory it's important to understand the meaning of anthropology. The term anthropology originates from the Greek anthrōpos meaning humankind; therefore, as an anthropologist my role is the study of humans past and present using the collective knowledge of archaeological, biological, cultural, linguistic, and social disciplines." Helen paused and looked at Aaron for several seconds to gauge his reactions before then continuing. "As you know Homo Sapiens Sapiens is the scientific classification for the human race or species and the only surviving species of the homo genus of which there were several human species coexisting until relatively recent times such as the Neanderthals."

Helen paused briefly to catch her breath and to curl some of her hair into place behind her ears. She caught sight of Aaron watching her every move. She wondered if Aaron had any feelings for her. She knew from the past how Aaron would flirt with all the girls at college and parties, but perhaps being older he had slowed down, she mused.

Pausing for a moment while she dealt with her hair she watched every eye movement from Aaron. With a cute smile she continued with her brief explanation of her theory.

"Recent DNA studies have found that most Europeans have between one percent and four percent of their genes inherited from the Neanderthals, so contrary to previous scientific understanding there were interbreeding between the two homo genera. The scientific establishment has only recently acknowledged this fact, before it was unthinkable for science to believe the possibility of such a suggestion," said Helen emphasizing her words with a tonal change in her voice.

"Oh, before I continue. Let's get the definition of 'species' clearly understood. A species defines the border at which an animal can interbreed. If two animals cannot breed then they are classed as separate species."

"I didn't know that…but it makes sense…physically the same species living together in the same environment are at some point are going to interbreed…its nature," said Aaron.

"I agree…you cannot argue against the proof of DNA evidence," agreed Helen.

"Aaron, I'm glad you said physically the same species…because for similar kind to interbreed they have to be of the same species…in this case Homo which really means humankind. That's why you don't see a fox breeding with a dog they are separate species and can't interbreed. But, the word 'species is often used incorrectly. That is why the Neanderthals were not a separate species as suggested by some people," said Helen.

"I still don't know what all this has to do with my quest, but, please continue."

"What is your quest?" asked Helen who was more intrigued to know Aaron's quest then continue with her lecture on the evolution of man.

"I'm not quite sure; it was something I heard the other day."

Aaron wasn't ready to reveal where he got the information for his quest. It was what the alien Iron Smart had said to him about being wrong concerning the evolution of man.

"There is much conjecture within the science community why there is a missing link in our evolutionary history as a species. Some argue that it's because archaeologists just haven't found the evidence yet. Their proposition is that bones decay relatively easy in acidic soils, so the evidence is difficult to find and that is why so few bone samples of early man survive. The science community is divided on what was our common ancestor; this is often referred to as the missing link in our evolutionary history."

Aaron listened intently as the professor was clearly enjoying her lecture. Only pausing occasionally, Helen had a gift in how she told a story.

"But, keep in mind there are also many missing links in the animal kingdom such as the missing link between fish and amphibians, you would have expected many different stages of development with a fossil record at each stage, but none have been found. Even Darwin was puzzled by this lack of fossil record, even though his theory of gradual changes of a species champions over a considerable amount of time, many millions of years that through 'Natural Selection' ultimately you derive a series of new species with a distant common ancestor. Now, you would expect to see the distinct changes in the fossil record, but we don't have those missing links."

"Perhaps, they haven't been found, yet," remarked Aaron and then immediately realizing he should have kept quiet. He was getting tired and felt the enormity of the last few days creep upon him like a dark shadow passing over him.

"If you believe in Darwin's theory then all life on this earth started with a single cell and then multicellular organisms evolved and these branched off into separate branches forming new organisms and so on, as explained in Darwin's tree of life. So, some of our genes in the Human Genome should not be unique as they would have to be inherited at each stage of our evolutionary development on the tree of life. So, why do we have a gene that is present in no other organism except humans called Fox –P2? Where did this gene come from, it exists in no other organism?

"I thought you said there is no such thing as genes?"

"Yes, that's true. Fox-p2 is a set of proteins we refer to as a gene," replied Helen.

Aaron keenly asked, "What is your theory, Helen? Please don't keep me in suspense you have hooked me line and sinker." As he said these words a huge smile came across his face and there was no escape like a fish hooked on a line as he waited for the *coup d'etat*.

"Although there have been published attempts through artificial insemination to crossbreed and produce a hybrid between our closest evolutionary relative the chimpanzee that has around ninety four percent identical DNA to humans the results so far have been unsuccessful." said Helen, before pausing to see the reaction from her audience.

"Yes, what is your theory, Helen," asked Aaron hoping for a *coup d'etat* or an end to the lecture. His patience was waning as the minutes ticked away.

"Okay, it's not my own theory, although, myself and many other leading scientists and anthropologists support the theory. The theory is called the Special Event Theory. The theory's proposition is that our intelligence and language abilities cannot be a product of evolution as described in Darwin's theory of Natural Selection because according to current archaeological discoveries they appeared to evolve in a relatively short space of time in evolutionary terms, and not the millions of years suggested by Darwin's theory of Natural Selection. Current archaeological discoveries suggest that man developed the ability to use sophisticated tools, and the ability to record their thoughts on cave walls, and one would assume the ability of language around 40,000 to 50,000 years ago. And, so what was so special then that all three abilities evolved at around the same time? Leading scientists and anthropologists argue that a special event must have taken place.

Helen continued explaining the Special Event Theory with a series of examples to further explain her argument on the plausibility of the theory.

"Can you see the enigma and the holes in Darwin's theory of evolution?" asked Helen. She could see from Aaron's facial expressions that he was not totally convinced. Helen waited for a reply from Aaron before moving on with the lecture.

Thinking for a moment before replying, Aaron stroked his beard with satisfaction. He was trying to collate in his mind what Helen had said and what she was inferring and what the alien Iron Smart had said. Somehow there is a connection between the two ideas. Perhaps, it's the Special Event Theory or some other event that played such an important part in man's evolution. He wasn't sure as he pondered what Helen had said. The only thing he was sure of was he was determined to find out the truth. The truth never lies, he said to himself.

"It's an interesting theory, Helen." Aaron could now see what the alien was suggesting. But, there is more as Aaron continued to ask Helen a lot more questions with a look of bewilderment on his face. He still wasn't sure what he was looking for, but he hoped he was now on the right track. He felt he just had to fit all the pieces together before he had the right answer much like a puzzle, he mused. Perhaps, that was the missing piece of the puzzle the Special Event Theory that Helen and her friends were proposing.

"Can I ask you...what are your reasons why you wanted to hear my theory?" asked Helen. Most people have a belief and they stick to it.

Aaron interrupted, "If I know there's a hidden message then I will find it. Now that I know what the theory is. Perhaps, now that I have this information I will be more likely to be open-minded during my quest."

"There is something else to consider," said Helen.

"What is that?" asked Aaron.

"Consider how human babies are so dependent on their mothers compared to other animals on the savanna where their young are born to stand and be able to run from the beginning not like human babies that are dependent on their mothers or someone else to look after them for many years before they can walk or run." Briefly pausing to look at Aaron's reaction Helen continued. "It doesn't make sense that our species are so dependent on their mothers. We are told that man's evolution started when we stood up and wandered the savanna in Africa. Yet, evolution suggests otherwise. Why do other animals born on the savanna have the ability to run from the word go? It doesn't make sense that we should evolve differently; after all we are only another animal. Evolution would have found a way of protecting new-borns with the ability to fend for itself or die."

"I can see the dilemma," said Aaron feeling more inclined to believe the doctor now that she had explained a major flaw in man's evolution.

"Can you see why Darwin's theory doesn't stack up? We have been told a lie. Because why would evolution miss such an important part of self-preservation. Again it makes no sense. Evolution takes millions of years. Yet, for some reason it forgot to protect our species. As if evolution didn't have to worry about being eaten by another predator on the African savanna. If you believe in Darwin's theory of Natural Selection then why do our species have no protection from predators? This paradox is an enigma that the scientific community cannot square. They choose instead to bury the facts and logic to continue with the status quo. But, there will be a time, when the truth cannot be hidden away and then people will see how far they have been misled by a theory that fits all, but it doesn't. We often make assumptions, which are often wrong and in the case of Darwin's theory it is wrong concerning man's evolution."

"I believe I understand what you're saying, Helen. It's like the old adage – you can't see the wood for the trees or something similar. My friend is trying to tell me something, but before he can I need to be open-minded to the possibilities," said Aaron smiling at Helen before continuing. "What the possibilities are, I'm not sure?"

Aaron thanked Helen for her time, and on the way back to the observatory continued with his thoughts on the merits or not of the Special Event Theory. There was something else, he wasn't quite sure what it was but was determined to find it. It was like an itch that just had to be scratched. It wasn't going away it nagged at him all the way back to the observatory. Perhaps, it was more important than the coming apocalypse, he said to himself.

***

Leaving the airport in his car, Aaron made his way back to the observatory. At first he hadn't noticed the black sedan that was following him. It wasn't until Aaron turned off the main highway onto the only road leading to the observatory that he spotted there was a car following him. He noticed there were two occupants in the car that was tailing him.

As the car got closer and out of the glare of the sun he saw it was a black sedan. He didn't know what make or model; it wasn't the sort of thing, he thought about. Aaron spent most of his time thinking about near earth objects or NEOs for short. He said many times to friends that we were more likely be hit by a NEO then winning the lottery. There have been many warning signs in the recent past, he explained. The explosion at Chelyabinsk, Russia highlighted our present vulnerability to NEOs now and in the near future. If that explosion at Chelyabinsk had not been in the atmosphere and actually hit the ground then it would have caused thousands of deaths rather than the thousands of injuries, which were mainly from broken window glass.

Aaron's fascination with NEOs began as a boy. He was coming home from school one day, when he saw a NEO streak across the sky. He could see the flames of fire as it quickly crossed close to earth. Aaron estimated from the height of the clouds in the sky that day that the NEO missed earth by around 10,000 feet. How big it was, he wasn't sure but the NEO was big enough to see red hot flames streaking across the sky. From that day his fascination blossomed and he studied anything and everything he could about NEOs.

Aaron at first thought perhaps it was tourists visiting the observatory. But it wasn't a visitor's day, as far as he could remember, he thought. The observatory often held visitor's day events for schools and colleges, but none were on the calendar for at least a month, he mused.

Frank had told Aaron and the other members of the group in Mongolia that government agencies were likely to start keeping taps on them. He hadn't thought it would be this quick. From his rear mirror he noticed the car tailing him getting closer and closer.

Aaron could almost see their faces in the mirror. He hadn't made any attempt to speed up. He hadn't done anything, as far as he was concerned and he had nothing to hide. As Aaron made a sharp turn around the bend of the mountain road the black sedan collided with his car's back bumper. Aaron's car spun like a spinning top before crashing into the road safety barrier. The black sedan also crashed into the barrier, but somehow somersaulted over the barrier and down the side of the mountain. Aaron saw the car burst into flames as it crash landed at the bottom of the mountain gorge. Viewing the scene from the edge of the crash barrier on the bend in the road, he reflected on his good luck.

In Aaron's mind, he was quite sure that he hadn't killed those men in the car. The actions of the men in that car had prevailed. They had killed themselves. He had no part in it, he said to himself. He knew how dangerous some parts of road could be; especially at speed the bends in the road could spin you off the road. As Aaron watched the smoke and fire of the explosion, he wondered what they were trying to do. He couldn't believe the notion that they were trying to push his car off the road and into the abyss. Whatever way he thought about the accident, he felt no qualms of guilt for the lives of the men who had been following him. Frank had warned the group that the government could do anything and that could mean killing the messengers, he remembered.

Without thinking, Aaron decided there wasn't anything he could do for those unlucky souls at the bottom of the mountain and promptly got into his car and continued his journey. He decided he would not tell Janet what happened as soon as he got to the observatory. He figured it was best not to alarm Janet. There was so much going around his mind, he wasn't sure at times where some of the information was taking him. The only thoughts had been staying alive.

Chapter 5

In a government department building close to 'Patriot's Avenue' situated in the government sector a secret meeting was taking place. At that secret meeting sat around a table were three government security directors. The government building was chosen as a safe house because of its location with its many different exits to the secure underground parking and its proximity to the White House and other government buildings. The room had previously been checked for surveillance devices and electronic bugs and had been cleared for use that morning.

"The WR104 protocol has been triggered and we must decide how we proceed," announced David Williams the CIA director to the other two men gathered around the table. David Williams was a career insider. He had spent his early youth in naval intelligence before working for the CIA. He was now past his best in physical fitness with fading blond hair and a pot belly to match his middle years. Clasping his dark rimmed spectacles he waited for a response to his proposal. He understood the implications of the WR104 protocol. He was one of the authors who originally drafted the protocol.

WR104 protocol had been a secret protocol since the days of the 'cold war' with Russia. The protocol had been set up to protect the national security of the USA and its allies, although America came first. At least that was the remit from its inception. At all costs, even if that meant retiring people permanently through any covert means if and where necessary. Whatever was necessary was sanctioned to safeguard the existence of the USA. The citizens of the USA owned the protocol, but only a handful of people would ever see the document that outlined the WR104 protocol.

IT was in 1967, during the 'Cold War' with Russia that the Americans stumbled on the biggest threat to the Earth and mankind. The USA had deployed satellites in space initially to listen and detect bursts of gamma rays by a nuclear explosion from Earth or in space. The Americans were making sure no one broke the recent treaty on the proliferation of nuclear weapons. But, scientists had a shock to find the gamma rays had come from a galaxy only twenty thousand light years away, relatively close in cosmology terms. The cosmic gamma rays had been travelling at close to the speed of light for twenty thousand years before they were detected by satellites orbiting the Earth. At only half that distance to the Earth, we would have seen mass extinctions, not seen, since, the mass extinction of the Permian period some 250 million years ago.

From previous mass extinctions scientists had noted that the prominent species of the period usually disappears, much like the disappearance of the dinosaurs around 65 million years ago from a NEO colliding with Earth. The dominant species in a mass extinction event ultimately dies and natural selection takes over. The disappearance of the dinosaurs allowed smaller animals to emerge, which led to the mammals filling that void and eventually the evolution of man.

A supernova explosion emits cosmic gamma rays that are the most violent explosions of highly energetic radiated particles that can strip the electrons from their atoms in your body. Most of life would be instantly destroyed in a few seconds of the gamma ray burst hitting Earth.

The WR104 protocol was set up to protect the American democracy in such an event. The cosmic gamma rays will hit the Earth on Wednesday 18th of June, 2029 with the centre of alignment over Africa. The exact alignment is within five percent degree of accuracy after many hours crunching data and numbers to arrive at the right longitude and latitude. The Earth facing the gamma rays would result in at least 50 percent of the Earth being decimated and destroyed from radiation. The types of radiation will destroy most life forms within seconds to days and the seas will see up to 90 percent of life destroyed. With up to 70 percent of all land life forms will also be destroyed.

"Do we know the persons of interest that have broken the protocol?" asked Simon Chandler the National Security Agency (NSA) director, who was quick to respond. Simon Chandler was an ex Federal Bureau of Investigation (FBI) agent, who had joined the NSA after leaving the FBI and gaining a law degree at Harvard university. Chandler on joining the NSA had worked his way to the top of the agency. He was now approaching retirement but still had an athletic build. His lanky torso and his blond hair that hadn't thinned or gone grey gave him the appearance of being younger, which sometimes made it difficult dealing with older subordinates. Many of his colleagues said that his dark green eyes were entrancing, which had a way of mesmerizing the observer. His main claim to fame was that he did everything by the book or at least that was the perception within the agency.

"Yes, we have all the culprits under surveillance," replied David Williams the CIA director.

"We have to decide whether to protect the protocol or somehow bury the truth for the sake of national security," said Jeremy Katz director of the Department of Homeland Security (DHS) who had a rich history as a former navy seal. After leaving the navy as a decorated war hero he joined the DHS as a field agent gaining rapid promotion before being promoted to director of Department of Homeland Security (DHS). Jeremy Katz lived on the edge with a constant anxiety of failure since his recent divorce from his college sweetheart. His dark olive skin and his brown eyes combined with his curly dark brown hair meant that he was often mistaken for an Arab. Born in Texas, America, he had inherited his Arab characteristics from his parents who had emigrated from Uzbekistan to America during the fall of the Union of Soviet Socialist Republics (USSR) in the early 1990s. Of the three men sat around the table, he was the youngest of the three. But, he also had had more experience than the other two in the field dealing with opponents of the American government, which made him feel superior to Williams and Chandler.

"I see one main problem," said Simon Chandler.

"What's that?" asked Jeremy Katz.

"The two CIA assets...Santoli and Khan can they be trusted to follow the protocol. I see from the initial report they have sworn the others to secrecy until they have secured a meeting with the President and the aliens. Their silence is not guaranteed," replied Chandler.

"I'm sure my men will do what they are ordered to do. I know Frank Santoli, he's a good man and a professional," replied David Williams head of the CIA.

"We are agreed then that the WR104 protocol continues as before even if we have to retire a few people for the greater good of national security," announced Katz.

The three men all agreed and that their meeting never took place. The WR104 protocol would continue for the sake of national security. The WR104 protocol was a top secret directive that limited the truth to a select few. Its purpose was the survival of the United States of America by any means, even if that meant the total destruction of countries or allies.

"We will meet again in a week's time at the Layfette safe house," announced Chandler. "In the meantime, we need to safeguard the protocol."

David Williams shook his head in agreement and made his way out of the building through a back door leading to the underground parking lot. The other two men also made their way out of the building to the parking lot separately without being seen. It would be the last time they would meet again at the same building. The building held a myriad of offices for small businesses so it was used as a convenient safe house close to the White House. The trio made a habit of changing their safe house for each time they arranged a meeting. There was less chance of being followed or the safe house being bugged.

Chapter 6

Ahmed Khan had been busy interrogating the CIA database system from his office at the Mongolian Department of the Interior. Located in a new building close to the city centre it was opposite the prestigious Hilton hotel. Frank Santoli had specifically asked for information related to WR104 and whether the aliens had warned humanity some twenty years before. Ahmed had also spoken on the telephone to arrange a meeting with a leading Mongolian astronomer and physicist called Professor Narnia Vechic. The meeting would take place at the University of Mongolia and provide for further background information on cosmic gamma rays.

***

On the drive over to the university Ahmed wondered what the professor would have to say. He already had his cover story why he was interested in cosmic gamma rays. Working at the Interior Ministry under the auspices of risk management it would come as no surprise to the professor why he was so interested in cosmic gamma rays? Although his usual remit dealt with natural resources, such as oil and its role in the economy combined with its effects on the environment within the state of Mongolia this was largely his cover job. The CIA had a way of covering their tracks within the labyrinth of government departments in any friendly foreign country. Frank Santoli had said to keep the investigation 'low key' and those were the words he had used. Ahmed knew he had to complete the task without the professor becoming suspicious of his real motives.

Ahmed's initial thoughts were turned upside down. Contrary to their telephone conversation his impression of Professor Narnia Vechic upon viewing her had completely changed. She looked no more than in her late teens to him. Her long straight black hair that caressed her shoulders also neatly framed her angelic face. He had mistaken her voice on the telephone to be from an older person and one he had associated with an ageing professor. Ahmed noticed the professor was surrounded by what seemed to him were large amounts of students' papers on her desk awaiting her perusal. It wasn't long before his CIA training kicked in and he was quickly reminded why he was in the professor's office? He politely introduced himself and thanked the professor for her time. Ahmed hoped she would be cooperative without being too inquisitive about his reasons for arranging the meeting.

Her head popped above her dark rimmed eye glasses as she scanned the man stood before her desk.

"We spoke on the telephone. You were in a hurry for information. That's why I agreed to this urgent meeting," remarked Professor Narnia Vechic with her deep brown eyes firmly locked on to the man stood before her desk.

"Please take a seat and we will see how I can help you," said the professor in a friendly manner.

As Ahmed looked across the professor's desk he was mesmerized by her Arabic looks with hair as dark as night. With almond skin and beautiful eyes that beguiled the viewer. She flicked her long hair that cradled the top of her back like a model does when seeking attention as she eagerly awaited the man's questions.

Ahmed placed a recording device on the desk and said, "This saves me having to take notes. So, I can listen to every word and understand what they mean at a later time."

"What can you tell me about cosmic gamma rays?" asked Ahmed leaning forward to stress the importance of the words.

"Why do you ask?" replied the professor with a question. She was like wasps protecting their hive and just waiting to pounce with a sting.

Ahmed had already thought ahead and had concocted a story to mask questions from the professor. As a trained CIA operative his responses would not arouse any alarm and would provide a natural exchange to any questions posed from the professor.

"I need to find out all I can on cosmic gamma rays because I'm creating a risk report for my superiors on potential risks for humanity. Other risks are Near Earth Objects such as asteroids and comets, volcanoes, and super massive coronal ejections from the Sun et cetera."

Ahmed explained that most of the threats are global in nature, but for the Mongolian government we need to understand the risks to the state and its economy.

"Okay, I understand. Well, cosmic gamma rays are ejected at the speed of light from some supernovae. These supernovas are the largest explosion of energy second only to the 'Big Bang' that we currently understand and observe in the universe. It's only since the 1960s that we really discovered cosmic gamma rays and that was by accident. Since the early 1960s and the proliferation of atomic weapons the Americans had decided to listen for gamma rays via their satellites and Earth bound detection systems. It was one day when the Americans picked up a burst of gamma rays that the Americans thought the Russians or the Chinese had exploded a nuclear weapon in outer space, but it wasn't them it was a burst of cosmic gamma rays that was picked up by their detection equipment from a nearby galaxy. Lucky for us on Earth the cosmic gamma rays had come from a galaxy some twelve thousand light years away, otherwise, it would be curtains for the Earth.

"What do you mean?" asked Ahmed.

"Well, cosmic gamma rays are the most powerful energetic radiated energy in the Cosmos. Any closer than about eight thousand light years then we would be in a serious situation. A super massive supernova that close ejects cosmic gamma rays that are highly radiated particles travelling at close to or at the speed of light. These particles would strip off our atmosphere and burn the Earth with radiation killing most of life in its path."

"Is there anything we could do?" asked Ahmed.

"No. If the supernova is close enough then we would witness a mass extinction of life under the path of the cosmic gamma rays. The width of the cosmic ray could be as wide as our solar system, so unless you are on the other side of the world as the rays pass you have no chance of surviving the gamma ray burst. Unless, of course you were thousands of feet underground as the rays pass over Earth," replied the professor.

"But, some people like miners may survive if they were deep enough underground say… several thousand feet. Is that right?" said Ahmed.

"Yes that is right. Is there anything else you would like to know?" asked the professor.

"How long would it take to pass by before it was safe?"

"At the speed of light only a few seconds, so half the Earth would survive, but then you have to consider the food supply chain, which would be devastating for the rest of the world. The food supply chain would be seriously diminished with half the world totally radiated. The ozone layer would be stripped away by the cosmic rays as it passes over the Earth. This would then lead to a weakening of our atmospheric protection from the sun. So, there would be a lot of problems for humanity for those that do survive the cosmic gamma rays such as decreased food supply, an increase in radiation from the sun and most likely a breakdown in law and order. We could also experience a global electrical magnetic pulse known as an EMP pulse, which could destroy much of the world's power grid throwing the world back a hundred years or more."

"But, why are cosmic gamma rays so deadly?" asked Ahmed.

The professor raised her eye glasses onto her forehead, as if she was getting bored with the conversation. "It's because of the type of particles ejected by the supernova, which are highly radiated and can strip the electrons from the atoms they encounter. These particles are called neutrinos and can go through solid rock as if it wasn't there. These neutrinos would turn essential organs in our bodies into mush."

"What do you know about WR104?" asked Ahmed realizing that the professor just may know some information unavailable on the Internet.

"Oh, yes I've heard about that star. It's a type one 'A' star. It's capable of producing a super massive supernova. It could go supernova at any time and we would not be able to do anything about it. It would devastate the Earth because of its proximity to us. It's relatively close in cosmic terms at around only eight thousand light years away."

"So, if WR104 went supernova eight thousand years ago its gamma rays would arrive here within the next few years, is that right?" asked Ahmed.

"Yes, those particles are travelling close to or at the speed of light. So in theory without crunching the data and the numbers the gamma ray burst would indeed shower the Earth in the very near future," replied the professor.

"Why are you so interested in WR104? It hasn't happened has it?" chuckled the professor continuing the reverse questioning. "Have you told me everything or are you holding back something?" asked the professor.

"I understand from the Internet that WR104 would pose a serious threat due to its proximity to the Earth and its angel of polarization. Essentially, the Earth is looking down the barrel of a gun," stated Ahmed with a confident tone in his voice.

"Yes, you seem to know a lot about this subject already?" asked the professor.

"Perhaps, more than I should have, but I like to be thorough in what I do," said Ahmed calmly as he stroked his beard. His thoughts had briefly returned to the dream that had kept him awake for much of the previous night. The dream had shocked him and made him aware that something wasn't quite right. That something was thousands of miles away on a different continent.

"Most people don't realize how dangerous the universe is and the more we find out the more dangerous it becomes. Everyone assumes that life continues without major changes to the environment and evolution."

"What do you mean?"

"Well, it's well known that the earth has survived many mass extinction events over its history and that around every 26 million years an event occurs. Over the past ten years we now know more about our universe and the dangerous events that are occurring on a daily basis somewhere in the universe. Cosmic gamma rays are at the top of the list, but just as destructive would be a large asteroid crashing to earth. A coronal mass ejection from our Sun could also do similar destruction to the Earth. A sudden climatic shift would also send us back to the stone age."

"What do you mean?"

"There is archaeological evidence to support the premise that the Earth has had sudden changes to its climate. Frozen Mammoths have been found intact with food in their mouths and bellies on the plains of Siberia. This evidence would suggest these animals were suddenly frozen on the spot, and a new ice age lasting thousands of years would begin," said the professor.

"A snowball Earth is the term used to describe the global effects of an ice age, which has resulted in several mass extinctions over the history of the Earth. Lucky, for us something survived, otherwise, we wouldn't be here according to current thinking," said the professor cutely as she smiled at Ahmed eagerly awaiting his response.

"What do you mean…current thinking?"

"Well, no one is sure about the evolution of life and how it got started and did it start from Earth or did it arrive here from other worlds? There is also the question of DNA. How did the structure of DNA evolve? Did DNA evolve here on Earth or was it brought here from another world via an asteroid or comet? You see the problem is DNA and how did it evolve? Solve that problem and you can easily calculate the number of worlds where life would be found. We have already surmised the possibility of life on several moons around other planets in our solar system. Go to other solar systems where life perhaps has had several hundred million or billions of years to evolve and perhaps you will find highly advanced intelligent life forms. Have you ever asked yourself why the Search for Extraterrestrial Intelligence (SETI) project hasn't found any intelligent communication since its launch in 1984?" asked the professor.

"No, I hadn't really thought about it before."

"Does this mean you believe in aliens?" Ahmed pressed on with the questions. His CIA training had it uses, when it came to interrogation techniques it was especially useful.

Ahmed noticed a cute smile had crept across her lips before she replied, "Yes, is the short answer. There is no reason to suppose just because we can think outside our consciousness that we are the only life form that can intelligently think for themselves in this universe. It's preposterous to think of any other conclusions. Darwin was partly right in his theory of 'natural selection' but he was also wrong at the same time. Think of it like this...without making assumptions, which will be harder than you think. Because we all make assumptions but invariably we are wrong, so we should not base our strategies on assumptions. Consider the SETI project to find extraterrestrial life in the universe. The project relies on detecting radio ways in outer space and in fifty years they haven't heard a word. Now, don't you think that is strange when we are told how old the universe is compared to Earth? There are potentially civilizations that are many billions of years old out there in space."

"So, what is your point?" asked Ahmed.

"The point is we should be getting signals from where ever we point our radio telescopes. There should be a sea of signals and there is nothing but silence.

"Can you see the logic of what I'm trying to tell you?"

"Yes, so what do you think?" asked Ahmed.

"It means alien life forms are either using another means of communication or we just don't understand what we are hearing. To us the radio signals add up to background noise, but it's possible it's all around us but we can't understand it. That's because we make too many assumptions about what constitutes a communication signal."

"I understand a lot more then I bargained for. The truth and logic of all this is above my pay grade," said Ahmed.

"But, can you now see how easy it is to fall into a trap in your thinking? We teach our students to think and study as the best way to learn, but as individuals we are a product of beliefs systems based on biases. We follow those paths most of our lives without understanding the implications," remarked Professor Narnia Vechic pausing for a moment to take a gulp of coffee before continuing.

"Now consider the genome. A genome is a set of genes, which are part of the building blocks to produce an organic or biological genome. In other words, the genome can be what makes you or what makes another animal or plant. First, what is a gene? A gene is a piece of DNA that allows a cell to reproduce itself from a set of instructions encoded within the DNA structure." The professor paused for a moment, before she continued her argument on the anomalies of life. "Are you following me, so far?" asked the professor.

"Yes, but explain what is a gene, again?" asked Ahmed.

"A gene is just a set of molecules encoded in such a way as to form proteins. It's an inert object or concept. It is what is done with these proteins that create life.

"Are you okay, so far?" said the professor eager to explain her argument.

"Yes, continue," replied Ahmed.

"You see there is no such thing as a gene that creates intelligence that is purely by luck. We are a product of our environment and how we are brought up by our parents."

"So, what is your point?" asked Ahmed.

"The evidence suggests the genome of every living thing is more complicated than we previously thought. So, the thought of aliens existing is not absurd it's more likely than you winning the lottery tomorrow," said the professor.

"Sorry, but I don't understand your point?" queried Ahmed.

"Consider the ascent of man, we are told our species started using stone tools around one million years ago. Now, around forty thousand years ago we were still using stone tools and painting cave art. You have to ask; why is it; that it took a million years before we learnt to extract metals from rock?"

"What happened around forty thousand years ago?" asked the professor.

"Is that your point?" asked Ahmed.

"Yes, something happened where we went from the Stone Age that lasted for a million years to the age of metals, which happened like a blink of an eye in evolutionary terms." said the professor.

Ahmed had felt the urge in his mind like a nagging doubt to tell the professor the truth. He couldn't avoid telling the professor, it was like his mind was being controlled, but it was so subtle that he felt no qualms to follow his thoughts.

"What about if WR104 has already exploded?" asked Ahmed.

"Is that the real reason you are here?" asked the professor.

"Yes, it will hit the Earth on Wednesday 18th of June, 2029 approximately two years from now." replied Ahmed.

"Finally the truth…it took some time, but finally you could not hold it back any longer. How did you find out this information, what was the source?"

"An alien called Iron Smart told me. It wasn't just me there…there was four other people there," replied Ahmed.

"He also claimed to have been to Earth before and warned the American government twenty years ago."

"Do you know where the gamma rays will hit the Earth?" asked the professor.

"The kill zone as the scientists have called it will see Africa and everything below and above this continent totally destroyed. The terminator line is where life will have some chance of survival, which is totally due to the curvature of the Earth. Any energetic particles would then have farther to travel through our atmosphere," replied Ahmed.

"It seems you have become confident on this subject?"

"Yes, but now I know more because of you, Narnia," replied Ahmed who now felt a physical attraction to the professor.

"We could all meet our maker any second. It all depends on the Space Time Continuum. That supernova explosion could have initiated a ripple in the Prime Space Time Continuum caused by the huge gravitational forces wielded by the gamma ray burst," said the professor.

"How would that make a difference?" asked Ahmed.

"Think of it like a sea wave…that suddenly turns inwards like the shape of a 'C' that is curved inward like you see on the surface of the sea in a fierce storm. This can allow you to cross vast distances in space in relatively short time scales. You have then crossed what Albert Einstein called Space Time. Think of space, like a piece of fabric that is stretched out with each planet's mass curving the fabric down, which is actually curving space. The huge gravitational forces of each piece of mass acting together along that fabric we call space time," replied the professor.

"So, you are saying that the cosmic rays took a shortcut?" asked Ahmed.

"Yes, that's right…took a shortcut. You can call it that, because what would have taken thousands of years to arrive here has now jumped space and time and can arrive in years rather than thousands of years. You can call it…a cosmic shortcut.

"Why is that we cannot see the supernova?" asked Ahmed.

"Yes, that's exactly why, because the gravitational wave distorts time and space to such an extent that what we see is an illusion to reality."

"Why do you think the alien was so concerned to warn us?" asked the professor.

"The alien said that intelligent life was rare in the galaxy and its master felt it necessary to warn mankind, so that the humankind would continue as a species," replied Ahmed.

"At least someone is thinking about us," remarked the professor.

"Yes, but now comes the responsibility of keeping silent until our group decides to go public with this information. Can you do that?" asked Ahmed.

"Yes, of course."

"Oh, by the way, you will be probably watched digitally. So, be careful what you do. The very word 'WR104' will flag many surveillance bots in cyber space. Don't mention a word of what I have told you to anyone else. This is to protect you and me, but especially you. If you don't say a word to anyone then you can't be tracked. It's a simple as that. But don't be surprised if you feel like you're being watched. That may happen because they are waiting for you to break silence," said Ahmed.

"Will I see you again?" asked the professor.

"Yes, I want to see you again. More than you realize. Somewhere in all this mess I feel close to you. I have totally disregarded my profession and allowed my feelings to determine my responses. I have said all there is to say. It's now up to you and what you do that counts," replied Ahmed.

***

"Hello, is that you Frank?" asked Ahmed.

"Yes, it's me. What have you got for me?" asked Frank Santoli the CIA agent.

"I'll know a lot more than I did yesterday, after visiting a professor at the university. I can understand why no one has picked up the obvious supernova. The explosion of the supernova created a ripple in space time allowing the cosmic gamma rays to reach Earth in the perceived time rather than the actual time. But, sooner rather than later the light from the supernova will be the brightest object in the night's sky. The world will know something is coming just before it burns half the world to destruction. There is also something else; I believe I'm under surveillance."

"You can expect it, ever since you started investigating the WR104 star system. There is a protocol that is in effect as I speak. I also have experienced the same."

"Oh, by the way, I feel I'm under the influence of another mind, namely, the alien Iron Smart," stated Ahmed.

"Yes, I feel the same experience," remarked Frank Santoli.

"Listen, nothing feels right, but we will wait and see what the 'chain of command' does with the information presented to them. If Iron Smart lands their spacecraft of the lawn of the White House there is nothing we can do about it. In the meantime, send me your report and I will endeavour to do my best to understand the Space Time Continuum. But, from what you say it's been easy to miss the biggest event in the universe," said Frank.

As Ahmed looked out the window of his office a storm was raging. The rain battered the window glass like the noise of walking on pebbles on a beach. The summer was gone and it was a time for cold winds to announce the approach of winter. The winds they call the Levant, which came from the east across the Altai Mountains and across the lands of Mongolia usually, preceded the winter. Ahmed had learned of many legends as a child associated with the Levant and the Mongolian people.

"Did you understand what I said?" asked Frank.

"Yes, Frank, I just drifted as my thoughts considered the weather outside the office."

"Look! Take care and like I said don't make any moves, unless, I tell you to. Is that understood?" asked Frank.

"Yes, of course," replied Ahmed.

As Frank's mobile disconnected a sharp chill ran up his back that felt like his hair would curl if he had any on his head. The people behind the WR104 protocol would possibly go the 'Full Monty' to silence some people and start to retire people quietly through methods of accident or suicide. He was a target along with the other members of the group who went aboard the alien's spacecraft and now they knew too much. It gave him a chill to think what this deep state organization will do to keep a secret. What would be the catalyst that they started killing people? They may kill the entire group to preserve the secret, it was obvious to Frank when it came they would not expect it. He was not a coward, but didn't plan on dying before he got to retire from the CIA. At least no one would act alone before the group had discussed the issues. At the meeting previously in Mongolia, he had already made plans on how the group would gather in the future.

Chapter 7

As Frank Santoli made his way through the heavy traffic along 'Patriots Avenue' his thoughts turned to the unexpected message he had received from his superior. Michael Stubbs a section chief of the CIA had arranged a meeting with the President that morning. Frank rationalized that his request to see the President had been approved right up the chain of command. This renewed his faith in democracy and perhaps much more, he would have to see what happens, he said to himself.

"I have read your report agent Santoli. What is your view on this matter? Should we see the alien?" asked the President of the United States.

Henry Adams the President could trace his ancestors back to the Founding Fathers of the United States. As a representative of the Democratic Party he had become popular amongst young voters for his steadfastness for always doing what was fair and right. Now, approaching his later years when most people had retired, he still had a bright mind and the physical ability to work long hours. Before becoming President, he was a successful senator for Virginia in the state where he was born. It was often said by friends that if he had a beard he would have resembled Abraham Lincoln with his deep set brown eyes and his lanky gait. Now, with thinning grey hair and an orange glow from too much sunshine, he had what most people would describe as a face that had character. The President had the type of face that was memorable and would not be out of place in a Sergio Leone Spaghetti Western film.

"Yes, you should see the alien. Since that report there is more information about WR104. But, it doesn't change the fact that these gamma rays will hit the Earth and according to our data analysis and the alien Iron Smart's calculations the whole of Africa and everything above and below will be burnt to a crisp," replied Frank Santoli.

"So, everything checks out…the alien is right. Perhaps, I should meet him," said the President.

Several of the people gathered around the table looked aghast that the President was willing to meet with the alien. The CIA director David Williams immediately warned against arranging a meeting with the alien, on the grounds that it could pose a biological threat to national security and its commander in chief.

"How do we know it's not just a ruse to kill you...Mr. President," said David Williams the CIA director.

The President nodded his head with agreement, and taking his time to respond. "You could be right, David, but this is the biggest catastrophe to hit this planet since the dinosaurs went extinct. So, I will meet with the alien, here, surrounded by my closest allies and friends. And we will see what the alien has to say. Perhaps, they can help us in some way. We will see. In the meantime, we have to make plans on how we deal with this issue on a global scale. When do we inform our neighbours and start evacuating people?" asked the President.

"Perhaps, we should do nothing...I mean don't inform those countries and yes, let those people die," said the CIA director.

"We can't do that, surely, we have a duty to inform those countries and the people that will be affected by these cosmic rays," said the President.

"Have you considered the impact this will have on North and South America? Number one will be food supply with decreased land for agriculture and with an increasing number of refugees from the other side of the world. We have to consider these issues," said Simon Chandler the National Security Agency director.

"But, our democracy is based on our Founding Fathers' belief we are all created equal under God. So, we cannot forget our brothers and sisters in Africa and the other countries affected," said the President.

Both Williams and Chandler tried their best to convince the President that it would be best to do nothing. They both cited the increased risk of civil disobedience, food shortages and doomsters. But, the President was adamant that this was the time to step up and that American must lead the free world in its approach to the issues, the President had argued. Many of the politicians gathered together in the Oval Office of the White House were amazed at the response from the President. The people present at the meeting had witnessed a President that was now a much more tolerate person. The president was opposite to his normal behaviour in subtle ways that was hard to see, yet, it was there to see. In the room, a mysterious person spoke up for the first time.

A Space Time Apocalypse

"Mr. President. You are right. We have no choice but to act as soon as possible. And more importantly, act in a way that helps rather than hinders progress. If we do not, we will never be able to say 'equal below God' and for all man. But, we have to forget we knew about this catastrophe twenty years ago, for the sake of mankind. We don't want to create a whole new number of enemies, so remember this is news to me. Otherwise, we doom our country into oblivion and democracy down the same dirty pipe," said Dr. Phoebe Gupta special adviser to the President.

"Yes, thanks for that, Dr. Gupta. I hear your concerns and we are on the same page," said the President.

"Arrange the meeting Santoli for midday, tomorrow!"

Arranging the meeting was the easy part, thought, Frank Santoli. But, he couldn't help to wonder if Iron Smart had other motives than what he had been told by the alien. There would be several security checks of the alien before the alien got anywhere near the President. That eased his mind somewhat, but there was a nagging doubt, he couldn't get rid of. He wasn't sure how far the 'deep state organization' whoever they were would go to keep a secret? Whatever, he did, he knew he was a target and that also included the other members of the group that first met the aliens in the Gobi desert.

The following day, Frank was watching the alien arrive on the Closed-Circuit Television (CCTV) at the rear of the White House. From his CCTV terminal screen, he watched as the alien was again checked by security guards for explosives, concealed weapons or any biological agents. Iron Smart looked unmoved by all the attention, but then again Iron Smart was just a machine, its artificial intelligence surpassed all Earth had to offer. Frank still had his doubts about the meeting with the President, but he couldn't help to wonder. The real reasons would soon be apparent and with good intentions, he hoped.

Iron Smart, looked just like you or your neighbour from a distance and could also change in an instant like a chameleon changes color. Iron Smart was not biological so had no feelings like humans, it was purely artificial intelligence and advanced mechanics. Frank could only wonder at what the alien was thinking, if it had any thoughts, he mused?

"This is the President of the United States of America," said the advisor.

"Good afternoon, that is what you say, is it not?" said Iron Smart.

Frank Santoli noticed the alien Iron Smart, sat down, opposite the President. The President was surrounded by several members of his cabinet, including the other members of Frank Santoli's group. All that had gathered in the Oval Office with the President were intrigued to know what the alien had to say to the President.

"I asked for this meeting, because we must save as much of mankind as possible. Life exists in most parts of the universe, but intelligent life that can explore the cosmos is rare. Our kind has a duty to help other worlds where the threat to mankind is real," said Iron Smart the alien.

"Do not worry! I have already made the decision to inform the countries involved. Even though, most of my cabinet is against my decision, I understand their worries over food supplies and more. But, we endeavour to excel in our ability to cope for the survival of the species. We must cope, it's as simple as that," said the President.

"You will cope!" said Iron Smart.

"Can you help in any way?" asked the President.

"We cannot stop the gamma ray blast. You will have to find ways of coping. Think of space more like a liquid. In the future, you will be able to travel to the stars. Currently, you think in the time frame of thousands of years to travel between stars. Try to imagine, a wave in the sea that can curl back, like a surfer rides the rip curl. Otherwise, without the rip curl there would be no momentum to propel the surfer forward with speed. At the end of the curl, we can transfer to a destination in less time than it would if we followed along the length of the curl. Now, can you see how we are able to warn you?" asked the alien Iron Smart.

Frank Santoli and his colleagues that first met the aliens were just astounded as were the President's advisors that had gathered to hear the alien. The three security directors that had kept the WR104 protocol secret were not persuaded to the President's or the alien's point of view. These three individuals that were responsible for keeping the WR104 protocol secret were already formulating plans to meet and discuss their next steps.

Frank Santoli, was surprised how easy it was to get this far. He had expected his request to arrange a meeting with the President and the alien would be blocked at every stage, yet, it had gone up the chain of command without any hiccups. This had puzzled him as soon as he heard the meeting had been arranged. It was just something in his mind, he couldn't work it out, but he knew it was there like a nagging person that never lets go, it was something that he'd been told.

"Yes, I believe I do have a better understanding of how we missed the clues to the cosmic blast," said the President.

"What will you do now?" asked the President.

"We will return home. We will arrive home quicker than you think, using the same techniques as I discussed earlier. Remember, think of space like a liquid and that black matter you theorize about comes clearer. And remember the gene is not the key," said the alien.

"We thank you for your help and we welcome your return," said the President.

Iron Smart was then escorted by White House security personal into a vehicle and driven back to its spacecraft, which was waiting only twenty miles North West from the White House in a clearing surrounded by a forest.

Frank Santoli and his group were then ushered from the Oval Office into an adjoining room where they could discuss their next moves. Frank had said it was better to behave normally and not allow the sister organization to act. Frank had said it was the best way to stay alive.

"Well, it's now up to the President. It looks like we have done our job. We can only hope that what follows before the blast hits Earth is something we can deal with. There is one thing that has bothered me right from the beginning. And that is how easy it was to see the President and how willing he was to follow what we all believe is right. I had imagined we could all be dead and the WR104 protocol continuing on without anyone knowing the truth," said Frank Santoli.

"What did Iron Smart mean…about the gene?" asked Professor Aaron Mikovitz.

"That's for you and others to figure out," replied Frank.

"Does that mean I can publish my story?" asked John Cramer the New York Times reporter.

"No, don't do anything and I mean not anything until the President makes an announcement. Otherwise, you could get killed," said Frank.

"Remember, don't be greedy! Wait until the President makes his move. Until then, we do nothing. We are all being watched, so we do nothing, remember that," said Frank

"Can we inform people we know about the blast?" asked Ahmed Khan.

"No, we keep quiet until the President speaks out," said Frank.

"What about if the President changes his mind or dies? What then?" asked Dr. Janet Taylor?

"We will decide on that bridge if we have to, until then, we do and say nothing. Is that all understood?" said Frank as he scanned the faces of his group. They all nodded their heads in turn affirming their decision to Frank.

"If you want to get in touch then use this encrypted text message service. I suggest we all download and load it now onto our mobile phones and register. We will use the username, Aaron-WR104 for you Aaron, and Janet-WR104 for you Janet, and so on? Do you understand? They will monitor our every move so don't give them anything to upset the apple cart. The encrypted text message service will allow us to communicate without anyone being able to decrypt the message. Just to make sure you have the usernames correct, we will all create a group, so that we can send messages to all members of our group. It's important that you all understand the risks that we may have to take should the President changes his mind," stated Frank.

"That won't happen will it? I mean the President has already agreed to inform the world," asked Janet.

"Anything could happen, nothing is certain in politics," replied Frank.

Suddenly, the door opened to the room and one of the President's secretaries said, "The President will see you now before you leave."

As the group stood before the President who was sat behind his mahogany antique Oval Office desk the President leaned forward and said, "Please do not publish anything on this cosmic gamma ray blast."

The group all agreed that they would wait for the President's announcement to the world before publishing anything. John Cramer said, "We will keep our side of the bargain."

Aaron said, "Mr President you have saved the world. We hope to save as much as possible."

The President retorted, "It was the easiest decision I've had to make and the right one."

As one of the President's secretaries shuffled Frank Santoli and his colleagues out of the Oval Office, David Williams looked on fearing the worst. The President was keen to embark on informing the world community as soon as possible. Before that could begin the President felt sleepy and headed straight for his private quarters and into bed.

Chapter 8

Meanwhile, the government security directors, whom had controlled the conspiracy surrounding the WR104 protocol was meeting in a safe house, not far, from Patriot's Avenue and only a few minutes' walk from the White House. All three had watched as the President could not be persuaded not to inform the world.

"What is our plan?" asked David Williams the CIA director.

"We have to safeguard America from catastrophe," replied Simon Chandler the NSA director.

"We all know the outcome should the President goes ahead. We have all read the studies and reports on how people will react," said Jeremy Katz director of the Department of Homeland Security.

"We will be labelled traitors if this ever gets out," stated David Williams.

"Has this ever happened before to a sitting President?" asked Jeremy Katz.

"Yes," replied Simon Chandler.

"I know it's playing the devil in one hand and playing God in the other. The more I think about what we are about to do the more I feel we have no choice, unless, we decide to go along with the President's idea. And that idea just doesn't seem practical the more I think about it. Let's imagine what happens after the blast. Over half the world will be living in North and South America, and that could be for a considerable amount of time, up to twenty to forty years before what was scorched by the blast will be safe to approach. We will have to learn to be less wasteful concerning food and learn to probably eat less. There are all kinds of scenarios where we just may cause a world war. I just don't think the President has thought through the complex issues and what may play out before we delve into the unknown."

As the other two waited for David to answer his mobile phone. "Yes, go on. Okay, let me know ASAP when anything changes."

"It seems the President is having a nap, apparently, he felt tired and retired to his apartment. He has called for a cabinet meeting at 8.15 this evening. This meeting will be our last chance to convince the President, so we need to show solidarity why it's not a good idea to inform the world of the blast? They will find out soon enough when the light from the cosmic blast will be the brightest light in the universe."

"Our other alternative is to take out the President without anyone realizing what is happening. We have previously discussed the means it is now up to us to act to safeguard America," said Jeremy Katz.

"What about the group who found the alien craft. What do we do with them?" asked David Williams.

"Well, it's a case of permanent retirement or we shall have to lock them up? Anyone of them could break the story wide open and we can't risk that happening, before we have had time to deal with the President," said Simon Chandler.

"The entire group is currently being watched twenty-four-seven. There are also a few more people we may have to deal with. It's those people that the group have been in touch with," said Jeremy.

"I think we could handle that without too much of a problem," replied the CIA chief.

"What about the reporter from the New York Times, he could be a major problem holding that lid down on the biggest story ever?" asked Jeremy Katz.

"We know he sent a file on the WR104 Protocol to his lawyer to be published in the event of his death or his will. We intercepted the file and removed it from his lawyer's office," said the CIA chief.

"I think its best we lock them up for a year until it's safe to release them. I don't feel comfortable prematurely retiring so many innocent people," said Jeremy Katz.

"I agree," said Simon Chandler.

The CIA chief said, "You are probably right, Jeremy. So we are agreed that Frank Santoli and his group should be detained until we decide it's safe? All three nodded in agreement. It's now up to the President and what he intends to do. We have our last chance tonight, otherwise, we have to act and disable the President."

"What options do we have?" asked Jeremy Katz.

"In the short term it would be simple for the President to suffer an illness that keeps him away from the public. But, the President of the United States of America is seen around the world as the leader of the most powerful country and so, it becomes difficult to keep him out of the way for any length of time," stated the CIA chief.

"So what do you propose we do?" asked Simon Chandler the NSA chief.

"We need time to formulate a plan, but in the meantime if need be the President can be given a mild case of flu, which will give us time to plan should we fail to persuade the President," said Jeremy Katz.

"What we are doing is safeguarding America," said the CIA chief.

***

Later that day, the three government security directors made their way separately in their chauffeur driven cars to the Whitehouse evening meeting. Inside the Whitehouse a CIA operative stood ready and waiting for the signal to act.

The President's cabinet included former generals, admirals and many previous stars in the financial world. The President's power was in some part controlled by just a few men and women. Most of the cabinet tended to be shy to the pressures of the press. If you asked the average American who the Secretary of the State was they would probably have no idea. Most Americans were too busy working and keeping a roof over their head most likely, thought David Williams the director of the CIA.

In the Oval Office the President's cabinet discussed the merits of informing the public for over an hour. During the discussion the cabinet were evenly split on whether to inform the public. The President listened to the debate keenly and after careful consideration reasoned that his original plan to inform the public was the best option available.

"I have listened to all arguments on this matter and have decided to proceed with my original plan to inform the public and all sovereign countries of the impending catastrophe," said the President.

There was an eerie silence around the room as they listened to their commander and chief continue. "It's now down to planning…we have to work out with other countries how we can handle the influx of refugees?"

"When do you plan to make an announcement, Mr. President?" asked the CIA chief David Williams.

"After we have informed our allies and briefed NATO, we shall inform the public," replied the President.

The President's reply was purposely non-specific, he had other matters on his mind, and he had started to feel unwell. The CIA agent had administered a flu virus to the President via a contaminated glass of water earlier that evening.

As the President closed the cabinet meeting, he also cancelled the following day's scheduled meetings with some of the top business leaders citing that he felt unwell. The President told his staff he would spend the time recuperating in his private residence at the White House.

Chapter 9

High up in the Appalachian mountains inside a log cabin, sat the three government security directors. They were there to discuss their next move after failing to convince the President of the merits of their plan.

"We have at best a few days before the President will be well enough to continue with his plans," said David Williams head of the CIA.

"Today, we must formulate a plan of action," said Simon Chandler head of the NSA.

"I only hope none of this gets back to us," said Jeremy Katz head of Homeland Security who was looking drawn with worry. Deep ridges had appeared along his forehead like the Grand Canyon of wrinkles.

"Don't worry…," said Williams. "We have nothing to fear, because this never happened. It's only us that can spoil the broth we are cooking."

"What options do we have?" asked Jeremy Katz.

"Our only option is to do whatever it takes to save America," replied Simon Chandler who gazed into the open hearth as the log fire crackled with flames. "We first need to isolate and arrest the group of individuals who could blow this story wide open. How is that going, David?"

"We have a list of individuals we think are dangerous to the stability and security of this nation. This constitutes the original group who first made contact with the alien and a few others. These individuals we think could pose a major problem to our plans and should not be free to talk."

"I'm glad you said arrest and not retire," said Simon Chandler.

"We all agreed last time we met that we would arrest them on charges of national security…," said Jeremy Katz.

Interrupting Katz, Williams restated his view, "Arresting them is the best outcome because we can control the information and the narrative that we would like to see."

"We have to make the President change his mind or we have to abandon our plans… Whatever we decide the sooner we arrest the group and close all channels to the WR104 project the better," said Simon Chandler who was busy pouring himself a tot of Brandy.

"Perhaps, you shouldn't be drinking when we have decisions to make," said Williams.

"Lighten up, David," replied Chandler.

"Perhaps, we should all have a drink," said Katz. As the three men discussed their plans, Katz and Chandler continued to enjoy the well-stocked bar, while Williams still refrained from drinking any alcohol.

"Option one, we convince the President of our plans or option two, we go along with the President's plan," said Williams.

"If we go with the President's plan then I don't see how America will survive," said Chandler.

"I agree with, Simon," said Katz. "If we go with the President's plan in its present form then I don't see how America will survive the apocalypse. Our country would disintegrate into total chaos. The rule of law would disappear and many people will die. Can we deal with the impending chaos that would ultimately in sue from the President's plan?"

"Our population would double virtually overnight and we have to plan and make sure our civilization can bear the burden, otherwise, we would only destroy the other half of the world that we are trying to defend. And that's no good for anyone," said Williams.

"It's no good feeding the poor if you can't eat yourself," remarked Chandler busy pouring himself another drink.

"We will have one more try at convincing the President, before we implement our second option. Are we all agreed," asked Williams.

Katz and Chandler both agreed. Both men nodded as Williams spoke on his mobile. "Arrest all on the agreed list and detain all to further notice. Report back ASAP," said Williams before ending the call.

"Within a couple of hours we should know our progress with the arrests and then we can make any decisions that arise," said Katz.

"Is that your agent at the White House?" asked Chandler busy downing another tot of brandy before Williams had a chance of replying.

"Yes. All is in play and the roundup and arrests have begun," said Williams reaching for a drink. He now felt he deserved a drink. The game was about to start and he was wandering how it would all end. Hopefully, for the good of the nation, he thought.

***

Peering through the front window venetian blinds Frank Santoli could see the shadowy outline of two men sat inside each of the two cars parked across the road from his second floor apartment. Frank had noticed the presence of being followed for several days. The CIA special training had alerted him before the government agents that were following him realized they had been made. Frank had purposely chosen to make no sudden moves and let whomever was following believe that Frank had no idea he was being followed. Reaching for his mobile he sent a prepared text message to everyone in the group that had first met the aliens in the Gobi desert.

Frank Santoli's only way out of the apartment without being seen would be via the bedroom window at the back of the apartment complex. From the bedroom window Frank lowered himself onto a porch roof and jumped into a neighbour's garden. Frank watched from the garden as the agents descended on his home. He then climbed over a garden fence and made his way onto the next street where he could then escape. The plan of escape had already been worked out long ago by Frank especially for this type of scenario. Frank made his way quietly into the next street without the agents realizing what had happened, before disappearing into the night.

***

"Hello. So far we have arrested everyone, except Frank Santoli, Ahmed Khan, Professor Aaron Mikovitz and Dr. Janet Taylor," said the voice on the mobile.

"Okay. Let me know ASAP when we have more information," said David Williams head of the CIA, as he ended the phone call.

"What's happening?" asked Jeremy Katz head of Department of Homeland Security who was supping his drink that had been warmed by the raging log fire.

"Yes, what's happening?" asked Simon Chandler head of the NSA, as if he knew something hadn't gone to plan.

"Four persons of interest have gone AWOL. I suspected possibly one of my agents could pose a problem and that would be Frank Santoli. I had him double teamed but he still got away," replied David Williams the head of the CIA.

"You train your agents well," remarked Katz with a sly grin on his face.

"What does this mean to our plan if we cannot capture these people?" asked Simon Chandler busy pouring another drink.

"We would be sunk if these people talk and they probably would talk," replied David Williams as he observed the expressions of worry on Katz's and Chandler's faces.

***

"Look at this new data I've found on WR104 star system," said Jamie the PHD student as he viewed the new data from his computer terminal. Continuing with the news, "It's definite that someone or some organization has been seriously messing with the data, Aaron."

It was already dark outside when Professor Aaron Mikovitz's mobile rang. Aaron glanced at the text message and knew straight away who the text message had come from and what it meant. The message read, "Meet at Joe's for dinner next weekend around 8pm. Text back if you can't make it."

The message was from Frank Santoli and it was a pre-prepared coded message that the group had to run for cover. The message had been agreed at the airport hotel in Mongolia should the need arise. Frank had warned the group that the government would try to arrest them. The message was part of the redundancy that Frank had spoken about. It warned the members of the group to immediately go into hiding should they receive the message from Frank.

Aaron and Dr. Janet Taylor were already aware that they were being followed and had been for several days. It was only a day after they got back from Mongolia that they began to notice the presence of a black Buick sedan with government registration plates that followed their every move around the clock. Aaron surmised that the two government agents sat in their car all day or night until they were relieved by other agents sometime during the day or night. Frank Santoli had warned the members of the group that this would probably happen and that they should be prepared to run for cover at any time. It would be up to each member of the group to find a suitable safe house and one that had no connection to them or any other member of the group. Frank had said to all the members of the group that this day would probably come and the use of a simple coded message would not alert a government digital surveillance operation until it was too late.

"That's great, Jamie," said Aaron as he quickly assembled his thoughts before continuing in his mind what he had to do. "I'll be back in a moment." Aaron hurriedly walked out of the observatory control room and down the corridor to Dr. Janet Taylor's office. Janet was already waiting for Aaron. Their escape route had already been planned. Frank Santoli had said to work out a suitable escape whether at home or work as these two environments would most likely be the scenarios that each member would face. All other scenarios would have to be dealt with on the fly without any preplanning. Frank had said they would have only a few minutes at most to evade any government agents.

"Are you ready?" asked Aaron as they walked out the back of the observatory's main building and got into a car they had borrowed from a friend purposely for this scenario.

Janet was already wearing the blond wig she had purchased for this occasion. "Yes. I'm always ready," retorted Janet smiling back at Aaron. Janet was just being precocious; it was part of her character since childhood.

"You look great. Let's get the hell out of here," muttered Aaron as he lay down below the car's dashboard on the passenger side. Janet took a cursory look to the right into the main carpark as she drove out onto the main road leading out from the observatory.

"Can you see them?" asked Aaron his voice slightly muffled by being cramped in the passenger well of the car.

"Yes. The agents are just getting out of their car and walking towards the front entrance," replied Janet before continuing. "Our ruse is working."

"Yes. Parking my car in the front carpark and always clearly visible to those agents day after day has gained us some valuable time to get to the safe house. Those agents have seen us arrive and leave in the same car since they started following us. Those agents are in no rush because they have been fooled into a false sense of security. They are not expecting us to run. And lucky for us, today, is a busy day, with a group of school children and adults visiting the observatory," said Aaron.

"Yes, you are right as ever," remarked Janet.

A Space Time Apocalypse

"People are coming in and out like flies around a carcass. So, those agents will not know what car we made our escape in and in a minute what direction we took at the junction with the main highway. And finding the safe house close to the observatory we can hide until we make our next move," retorted Aaron happy that their plan was working.

"Frank was right about the need to make plans for this day, otherwise, the situation at the observatory would have made it virtually impossible to escape from these government agents," stated Janet as she turned off the main highway onto a dirt track hidden from anyone driving up or down the highway.

The dirt tracks led from a busy truck stop to the outskirts of the nearest town. It was there that a friend not connected with the machinations of the observatory had offered the use of his home while he was away working aboard. Aron and Janet had purposely chosen an underground carpark that had limited CCTV, which was ideal for the switch of vehicles. This was necessary Frank Santoli had said because the government would use every means possible to find them. Frank had told the members of the group that it would not be easy to evade the government security agencies regardless of which one it was that would be tracking them. But, Frank had stressed that it was now possible to keep several steps ahead of the government provided they didn't use anything that would leave a digital footprint. That included mobile phones, credit cards or anything that could leave a digital footprint.

All communication between members of the group had previously been discussed and decided on at the airport hotel in Mongolia. Communication by phone between members had to follow a strict set of rules that Frank Santoli had devised. Provided members of the group followed those rules then it would be difficult if not impossible for the government to track their mobile phone communication. Frank had told Aaron and Janet to buy another mobile that was pay as you go and could not be tracked if it was used correctly.

The safe house had a garage where the car they were driving could be stored away from prying eyes. Aaron and Janet felt the house was a perfect hideaway. The house was tucked away at the end of a quiet cul-de-sac surrounded by forest for miles. The nearest neighbour was at least a quarter of a mile away. And because the house was situated in a gated community with security guards at the entrance the neighbours would be far less inquisitive about any activity at the house.

"Finally, we have made it," announced Aaron holding a glass of wine already more than satisfied they had escaped the clutches of the government agents. "Shall, we make a toast that whatever happens in the future that we stick together and that we will get through this."

"I hope you are right about this being a good safe house, otherwise, we are going to spend some time twiddling our thumbs in an overcrowded prison," responded Janet as she raised a glass of red wine to her lips with a cute smile across her face.

***

Meanwhile, Ahmed Khan one of the five who had witnessed what the alien Iron Smart had said aboard its spacecraft had just received the coded text message from his boss Frank Santoli. It was around 3.am local time in the capital with most people still asleep in Mongolia. Ahmed knew he had little time to waste as he quickly got dressed and grabbed his 'Go Bag' before looking out the front window of his apartment. Ahmed noticed that the black Skoda sedan was parked at least around 50 meters from his high rise apartment block. The car and the people inside it had been following him for most of the day and night for the past couple of days.

If he timed it right, he could be downstairs and waiting for the agents to get into the escalator as he made his way to the resident's carpark without the agents seeing him escape their clutches, he mused.

Ahmed had kept a small table light on in the living room when he was home, so that the agents felt comfortable everything was normal. He closed the door to his apartment just as the agents were exiting their car; with the table light on the agents would believe Ahmed was at home sleeping, he mused.

As Ahmed had expected both the agents used the lift to get to the 8th floor neither one of them willing to take the stairs and cut off a possible escape using the internal fire exit stairs. His ruse had worked. The agents there to arrest him were probably low level Mongolian police helping out the CIA, he surmised. This had helped in his escape via the rear of the apartment block, enabling him to walk around the corner to another apartment block carpark. The carpark was situated approximately a quarter of a mile down the road heading south, where he had recently acquired another car ready and parked for such an occasion.

As Ahmed drove the car into the long stay carpark at the Mongolian airport, he knew he was nearly there. He caught a bus and crossed the border into Kazakhstan and made his way to the safe house he had previously picked out. The safe house was above a convenience shop located close to a nearby transit hub for travellers seeking convenient access to local buses, trains and planes.

He sat down on the bed and grabbed the mobile phone from the 'Go Bag' and checked the only phone number stored on the phone. He had already discarded his normal mobile phone on the motorway. It was a rule that his boss had already told all members of the group to do. Frank had said, "After you get the text message to get to a safe house, discard your old mobile phone."

Frank Santoli had made sure that each member of the 'alien five' a phrase he sometimes used to refer to the group knew the consequences that could happen if someone didn't follow the rules. It will be easy for government agents to track our movements, it was that simple, Frank had said to the group, Ahmed had remembered.

The 'Go Bag' Ahmed had assembled contained other essential items such as a First Aid Kit, compass, lighter and other items such as dry fire starters. It was light to carry and important for any survivalist to have.

Ahmed lay on the bed waiting for the mobile to ring, he considered the steps he had taken to stay hidden and off the radar. At this moment, he had no digital footprint, he would be totally elusive as 'Big Foot' is today in the world. Ahmed had setup a communication channel between Frank's new mobile and his.

***

The next day, Ahmed Khan had arranged to meet Professor Narnia Vechic in Mongolia near the border with Kazakhstan. They took a bus to the prearranged meeting place with the desert nomads. Ahmed and Narnia saw the group of nomads sat round a camp fire trying to keep warm waiting for them to arrive.

"Are you ready to go?" asked Ahmed.

"Yes, Ahmed, we are...when you are ready," replied the nomadic tribe person with a lisp on every word. Ahmed noticed that the man had few teeth to bark orders to his men, but, he was their leader.

"My men are always ready," said the nomad leader.

"Good, then let's get going," replied Ahmed eager to get to his destination.

Ahmed and Narnia mounted their camels with the help from the nomads and followed the camel train into the desert. The sunrise had just begun, so it was partially dark. The previous night had not yet ended.

For Ahmed and Narnia, it was their first time riding a camel, so they both made themselves comfortable the best they could. Ahmed had explained to Narnia that the journey to their destination would take about two to three days depending weather conditions.

It was several hours before the heat of the sun soon made the sweat pour down Ahmed's face. The *keffiyeh's* Ahmed and Narnia were both wearing stopped most of the sweat, but not all. It was essential clothing to mask the sun's rays against the heat of the day. Anyone seeing the camel train would think it was just another nomadic tribe moving through the Mongolian desert. The leader of the camel train had said to Ahmed that it would be the winds that would test their resolve. He had said that many people had died in the desert because they went mad without water and not knowing where they were. But, for the nomads it was easy, they never found themselves without access to water and understood where they were. The nomad leader never explained to Ahmed the secret of their survival. It was there secret and they wanted to keep it that way.

The wind was starting to pick up. Ahmed saw how the vultures circling above kept pace with the camel train. You could hear the birds' cries and shrieks every few minutes, as if to say we are following you, he mused. His thoughts turned to what the alien Iron Smart had said. The world is about to be hit by a cosmic gamma ray burst that will kill everything in its path. But, there is hope for the world. Those were the alien's words. He hoped the alien had been sincere, otherwise, it's fifty, fifty, who lives and who dies, he said to himself.

The sound of the howling wind reminded Ahmed of a terrifying sound from a horror film. At times, he felt the cold of the wind chill his body as if someone had poured cold water over his body.

Shouting to be heard over the relentless noise of the wind howling like a demented soul, the nomad leader said, "The wind is getting stronger. We will camp over there near that outcrop of stone and wait for the winds to go."

"Okay, whatever you think is best," replied Ahmed.

"Good, I could do with a rest from this saddle and the camel," remarked Narnia.

"Yes, I feel the same."

As the camel train made camp the winds had taken over. It was difficult to be heard above the relentless sound of the wind. Behind an outcrop of stone and sand dunes the camel train was protected from the worst of the winds. Ahmed watched as the nomads made fire and cooked their food. The nomad leader spoke in a nomadic language to his men that Ahmed and Narnia could not understand.

"What are you saying to your men?" asked Ahmed.

"I'm telling them a story," replied the nomad leader with a lisp on every word. "We exchange stories whenever we can."

"Can you translate and tell Narnia and I?" asked Ahmed.

"Yes, I will," said the nomad leader.

"The story starts in the days of the Mongol empire. Early in the twelve century there lived a prince. The prince was called Pashanpour. His father shielded Pashanpour, from most of the outside world. But, Pashanpour had a man servant, who would tell the prince about the world his father had tried so hard to hide," said Ali the nomad leader.

Ali explained that one day a blind man arrived at the palace gates with a donkey carrying pots and pans. The blind man asked to see the prince's father, but was told that he was away dealing with other business, so the prince reluctantly had a parlay with the blind man.

"The blind man told the prince that, tomorrow, he would travel to Vladivostok on the coast with his trusted donkey. The prince also said that he and his servant would be travelling to the same city. The blind man offered the prince the chance to travel with him. He told the prince that he had travelled many times to the city across the desert and never got lost. The blind man told the price that it was dangerous to cross the desert without the skills to do so."

"Sounds like a good story, so far," remarked Ahmed, ready and waiting to clap the nomad leader who was called Ali.

"The prince wasn't used to taking advice from such a lowly subject such as a blind man selling pots and pans. The prince declined the offer, but offered to carry what the blind man's donkey was carrying, so that the blind man didn't have to walk beside his donkey. At the same time the prince made a bet with the blind man that he would arrive first in the city."

The nomad leader continued and said that the prince and his servant set off on their camels the following day for the city. The blind man followed the prince on his donkey. The blind man on his donkey tried to keep up with the prince and their camels. But, before long the prince and his servant could not be heard by the blind man. The blind man wasn't concerned he would lose the bet. The journey to the city would take several days even on camels, the blind man surmised.

"On the second day of the blind man's journey a fierce sand storm began, so they stopped and waited out the storm. The blind man knew it was the safest thing to do. Meanwhile, the prince and his servant tried to stay together, but they got lost in the storm," said Ali.

"When the blind man reached the city he waited for days for the prince to arrive, but he never did. The prince's father had several searches conducted, but no trace of the prince or the servant was ever found."

"Excellent, that was excellent," remarked Ahmed as he clapped hands with everyone gathered around the camp fire. Ahmed noticed a big smile on the professor's face. She had also enjoyed the camp fire story, he mused.

"Do you understand the morale of the story?" asked Ali the nomad leader.

"Yes, I believe I do," replied Ahmed.

"Tomorrow, we cross the Mongolian steppe. Famous for the Mongol horse that roamed these lands," said Ali.

"Yes, the horse that Genghis Khan and his Mongols used to build an empire," interjected Ahmed.

"A different breed that didn't need expensive feed, it could feed and survive on what the steppe had to offer."

"You know a lot about Genghis Khan?" asked Ali.

"Probably more than most…because of the life and times of Genghis Khan who is a national icon in Mongolia," replied Ahmed.

"Perhaps, tomorrow, I will tell you and your men a story. We will see."

"In the meantime, Professor Narnia Vechic and I are ready for some sleep."

As Ahmed and Narnia gazed up to the night's sky and viewed the wonder of the Milky Way. Ahmed said, "Somewhere up there in the stars lives Iron Smart."

"Don't you think it's strange we have not heard from the President?" asked Narnia.

"Yes and no. Perhaps, there are reasons why, but, we are not privy to the reasons?" replied Ahmed.

"I guess you are right."

"Let's get some sleep. We have to be up early in the morning."

Ahmed and Narnia crawled into their small tent. With their arms wrapped around each other they quickly fell asleep. It was the first time since joining the camel train that they had had time to be affectionate with each other.

The following morning, it was night, when the nomad leader called out to Ahmed and Narnia. Ahmed and Narnia could hear the voices of the nomads talking while having their breakfast. Ahmed and Narnia were lucky that the nomads had saved some coffee for them. There was no time to waste, before the camel train was on its way again.

"This place we are going to…what is it?" asked Narnia.

"I told you before; it's an abandoned Christian church. But, now, it's just a home of a friend."

Ahmed continued, "It will make an ideal safe house."

"It's certainly out of the way…how long before we get there?" asked Narnia.

"We should get there in about two days."

"Let's hope it's as safe as you expect it to be," stated Narnia.

As the camel train crossed a small valley between two small hills the nomad leader stopped and waited for Ahmed Khan and Professor Narnia Vechic on their camels to catch up.

Pointing to a distant mountain on the horizon, the nomad leader said, "Look! At the mountain in the distance… that mountain is sacred. It is said that Genghis Khan is buried somewhere on that mountain."

The nomad leader continued, "No one has found the burial site. No one is allowed to dig there."

The nomad leader continued to explain how important the mountain was to the Mongolian people.

Pointing, at the professor's camel, the nomad leader said, "Oh, by the way, the camel you are riding is called Tasmin. The camel is female and is sometimes difficult to handle. But, Tasmin produces a lot of milk for us to use, so we put up with her ways."

"What about my camel does it have a name?" asked Ahmed.

"Yes, all our camels have names. The camel you are riding is called Benny. I don't know why we called it Benny?" replied the nomad leader.

Ahmed and Narnia could feel the heat of the sun through their clothes. The occasional distant sound of a shrieking bird was all they could hear. The desert wind would provide an occasional cool breeze, but, there were no other sounds to distract them from their journey. If it wasn't for the vultures high above in the sky circling their camel train there would be no other sounds other than the grunts and groans of the camels, he mused.

Later that day, they made camp near a dried up river bed. It didn't take long before the sun started to set. Everyone huddled around the camp fire trying to keep warm from the cold of the night. The nomads listened to their leader once again telling a story.

"Would you like to tell a story, Ahmed," asked Ali the nomad leader.

"Let me think for moment. Perhaps, Professor Narnia Vechic would like to tell a story?" asked Ahmed.

"Okay, I will. This story was told to me when I was a little girl. I was told that the story was a true story. It all begins in a prison cell beneath an old castle. The castle was the home of an important king. It was said that the king kept all the gold and riches there that the king had won in previous battles.

One day, a man dressed like a beggar came to the court of the king. The beggar said to the king where is your gold? The king told the beggar that the gold and all his wealth were safely stored in a dungeon deep below the castle. The king said the dungeon was guarded day and night by his trusted soldiers. The beggar told the king to go to the dungeon where the gold was stashed. The beggar told the king that his wealth had gone. The king laughed at the beggar and told him to follow and I will show you. The king and the beggar made their way down to the dungeon.

When the king and the beggar arrived outside the dungeon they both saw two soldiers that were guarding the door to the dungeon. The soldiers were shocked to see the king, because the king usually never frequented the dungeon. The king demanded the soldiers open the door to the dungeon. When the door was opened the dungeon was bare. The gold and all the riches had disappeared. The king roared in anger that heads would fall. The king asked the soldiers if anyone had been inside the dungeon, only, the king they said. The king then asked the beggar what he knew, only, to find the beggar had already said the gold was gone. The beggar then said the gold was payment for the king's life. The king asked the beggar what he meant. The beggar said to the king that he would see his daughter marry in three months' time. The king was puzzled and had the beggar arrested.

Back in the castle's court, the king asked the beggar how he stole his gold. The beggar told the king that where he was going that gold and money had no value. The king asked the beggar's name. The beggar replied that they call me the 'messenger' and turned away and duly vanished, as if he was never there.

Three months later the king's daughter was married and shortly after that the king died," said Narnia.

"That was a good story," said Ali the nomad leader.

Everyone present clapped to show their appreciation of the professor's story. At that moment, Ahmed looked up at the night's sky, which was clear of clouds. The Milky Way was visible in all its glory. Shrieking across the sky, Ahmed saw what looked like an UFO.

"Look!"

Pointing to the direction with one hand, Ahmed said, "We are not alone in this world."

"Yes, I can see that...it looks enormous. I can see lights, which are flashing on and off in different colors. There are red, blue and yellow lights around the centre of the UFO," remarked Narnia.

"Yes, I can also see the spacecraft," muttered the nomad leader with every word mumbled from the trembling of his body in the cold wind.

Ahmed already knew about the existence of UFOs and aliens and wasn't shocked by their appearance in the night's sky.

He had already convinced Narnia of their existence. The nomads also were not alarmed to see the UFO. Ali explained to Ahmed and Narnia that on many occasions in the desert they had seen UFOs crossing the night's sky. He went on to explain that the UFOs came in different sizes and shapes, some were cigar-shaped and others were saucer-shaped. Ali explained that they never reported seeing UFOs to the authorities because they feared being ridiculed.

"I wonder where the UFO is going?" asked Ahmed rhetorically not expecting a reply from anyone. He was just thinking out loud.

Ahmed thoughts soon turned to what the alien Iron Smart had said about the coming catastrophe the planet faced. In Ahmed's mind, there were a lot of problems the world would have to face. If Iron Smart was right and its calculations were correct then this part of the planet would face total annihilation. The world would be in the hands of a few important people. It would be the American President's plan to save the planet. Yet, the world at large was ignorant of the coming disaster and the alien's message to save the lives of millions of people. How would the world react to these events, he wasn't sure.

"You seem to be in another world," said Narnia.

"I was for a moment," remarked Ahmed.

"I'm getting cold and ready for the tent," said Narnia.

"Yes, let's get some sleep. We have an early start again, tomorrow."

Ahmed and Narnia didn't feel the need to explain to each other why they felt uncomfortable making love in their tent. The prospect of making love didn't appeal to them, because of the number of men in close proximity of their tent. They would wait until they arrived at their destination. Cuddled together they fell asleep in each other's arms with only the sound of the wind that flapped against their tent as witness to their love for each other.

Ahmed was awake the following morning before Ali's call to wake up. With his arms still wrapped around Narnia, Ahmed thoughts were about how quickly he had fallen in love with the woman beside him. It was strange at the time how easy it was for him to reveal to Narnia the truth about what was about to happen to the planet. At the time, he had no qualms about telling her the truth, as if his mind was being manipulated in some form. He had felt something, but it wasn't just love that made him reveal the truth, he said to himself. Perhaps, the alien Iron Smart had something to do with it? He mused.

After breakfast, the camel train continued on its journey. Ahmed noticed it wasn't long before he saw a vulture circling their camel train. These birds that prey on carrion, he mused, must have a sense that anything travelling through the desert must be mad. So, these vultures wait for something to happen. They were opportunists like him, he said to himself.

"Did you see Tasmin being milked this morning," asked Narnia.

"What? Oh yes…the camel…your camel," replied Ahmed.

As the camel train trekked over sand dunes and along valleys for much of the day, Ahmed and Narnia were unaware they were close to part of the fabled 'Silk Road' popularised by Marco Polo the explorer. In the distance they caught sight of a camel train making its way east.

"A camel train is going east," muttered Ali as he signalled with his arm to his colleagues.

"When do we arrive at the church?" cried out Ahmed who was shouting at Ali, now several camels ahead of him. Ali raised his arm and displayed two fingers for two hours. Ahmed and Narnia were glad their journey to the church was nearly over. The camel ride at times was uncomfortable, especially, when there was no breeze to cool them from the scorching sun.

It was early evening, when Ahmed saw the first sign of the church. He could see the sign of the cross above a hill in the distance. The church would have been a welcome sight to pilgrims who were travelling along the 'Silk Road' for the first time, he mused. As the camel train got closer and closer to the church he saw what looked like broken red clay roof tiles scattered on the desert floor. He surmised the roof tiles had blown off the roof of the church in a storm. As they approached the gate to the building, Ahmed could see his friend, Felix.

"I hope you had a good journey?" shouted Felix.

"We did," shouted Ahmed who was at the back of the camel train with Narnia.

"Please, you are welcome. Come in," gestured Felix with his hands to the nomads and their leader Ali.

"You are welcome to pitch your tents here, tonight," said Felix to Ali.

"Felix, my friend, I hope you are well?" asked Ahmed as Narnia waited to be introduced.

"This is Professor Narnia Vechic, Felix. I hope everything is prepared for our stay?" asked Ahmed.

"Yes, of course. I have been busy since I received your message," replied Felix.

Felix O'Rourke had been a priest when Ahmed first became friends. Over the past ten years they had kept in touch. Felix had spent a lifetime as a priest before retiring and living as a recluse in an abandoned former Christian monastery. Born in Dublin, Ireland during the Second World War to devout catholic parents, life as a child was tough existing on food rations, he was always hungry, he would say to friends.

After leaving college, Felix joined a monastic order and was eventually posted to a monastery based in Cairo, Egypt. Felix was as tall and lean as Ahmed with a bald head and a Roman nose with dark brown eyes. Since, Felix's retirement he had grown a beard, which was now long and silvery in color.

Ahmed had first met with Felix in Cairo during the religious riots of the 'Arab Spring' uprising. Ahmed had been sent to Cairo to assist another CIA agent in his mission. During the riots, many Christian churches and monasteries were attacked and burned. Ahmed happened to be close by when Felix's monastery was attacked by Arab fundamentalists. Seeing this occurring, Ahmed managed to gain entry to the monastery and save the life of Felix. Since that day, Ahmed and Felix had become good friends and had kept in touch via mail.

***

John Cramer the news reporter for the New York Times was at home in New York getting ready for the day when he received the text message from Frank Santoli. He knew he didn't have much time, if any to spare. Frank had briefed everyone in the group about what could happen and how to avoid capture. Frank was quite specific about how a few seconds could be the difference between not getting arrested and getting away to a safe house. As John turned off his mobile and grabbed his 'Go bag' and preceded to the fire escape at the back of his apartment building he hoped no one was watching the back of the building. John's escape would depend on him reaching the underground substation, which was two blocks away from his apartment building situated in the 'Village' area of Manhattan.

Clutching his 'Go bag' John made his way down the fire escape into the alley adjacent to the building as quickly as he could without making too much noise and alerting other residents in the apartment block. It was raining heavily, which masked the noise he was making traversing the fire escape to the alley below. He hoped the government agents that had been following him for several days had not bothered to watch the back of the building, otherwise, his escape would come to a full stop. The car lights that suddenly blinded his vision were a bad omen, he thought. The government agents had indeed watched the back of the apartment block as well as the front.

"You're under arrest."

Before John could reply, he was put into the back seat of a car and a hood was placed over his head. He could feel the presence of another person sat beside him, but he couldn't see anything. As the car drove away from the apartment building, John felt pleased that he had taken the precaution of safely storing the story of the alien and coming catastrophe with his lawyer. He felt confident that sooner or later the story would be published should anything happen to him. Frank Santoli and the other members of the group had convinced him that this was the safest method of preserving the story.

"Where are you taking me?"

"Don't worry you are in safe hands," came the reply from one of the government agents in the car. John could not tell who was speaking, but assumed whoever it was needed answers.

"Why have I been arrested?" asked John Cramer his voice slightly muffled by the hood over his head.

"National security and you are a person of interest," replied the agent with a mid-western accent. "Why did you run?"

John thought for a moment before answering. He knew they already had his mobile and could easily check for any messages. "Perhaps, you can tell me where we are going?"

As the car got closer to Guardia airport John could hear the sound of airplanes landing and taking off in the distance. The next thing John felt was a puncture prick on his left arm. Within seconds John was asleep and comfortable until he was awoken sat inside a room with no windows. The room had one large rectangular secret mirror. Opposite John sat two broad set males. The men looked like ex-military types with 'Jarhead' style hair, which resembled the look of a jam jar.

"This is Wallace and my name is Stevens. We are both government agents here to interview you. We hope that you will cooperate with us; otherwise, this could get ugly. Meaning your treatment here will depend on your answers and your willingness to collaborate," said agent Stevens.

"Who do you work for?" asked John directing his question to Stevens who seemed to be in charge. The agent Stevens sounded like a New Yorker with a Brooklyn accent, thought John. The agent Stevens quickly responded.

"We both work for Homeland Security, but this is a joint effort with other agencies," replied the agent calling himself Stevens. "Now…why did you run?"

John paused for a moment and considered his answer. "Because we thought this could happen…that is…the government willing to cover up the story and willing to arrest us. So, we devised a plan of action. Frank Santoli and the other members of the group would get to a safe house until we heard different. My safe house was to be a friend's apartment in New Jersey."

"Your friends in this group all have different safe houses, is that correct?"

"Yes. We all have different safe houses. Each one does not know the others' hideout," replied John.

"So, you do not know the whereabouts of any other member of the group? Is that correct?" asked agent Stevens.

"No. Perhaps you have arrested one or two," replied John.

The two agents looked at each other in disbelief. Stevens looked down at a file in front of him and said, "Who else have you told about this encounter with the alien?"

"No one else, that's the truth," said John.

"That's not true. You are lying. You made two copies of the story about the alien and printed them. We have checked your computer and know the truth," replied Stevens.

"How long have I been here?" asked John in disbelief that the government knew so much, and so quick.

"Where are the copies?"

"Where you can't find them…and I'm not going to tell you," replied John smiling at Stevens as if he had the upper hand. He wasn't about to tell the truth. John had a wide smile across his face like a cat waiting to be petted. He knew they wanted answers. John felt that he had the upper hand. He needed concessions. "I want some food and drink, before I talk anymore."

"Okay. That's sounds reasonable. We all need some refreshments." Turning to his partner Stevens, he continued, "Go out and arrange some refreshments. Oh, and remember, Wallace, no red sauce on my burger."

"You don't like red sauce?"

"On contrary, I like red sauce, but I prefer my burger fresh. Not something cooked hours ago. It's the only way, I can guarantee a freshly cooked burger," responded Stevens grinning from cheek to cheek at John Cramer.

"Can I see a lawyer?" asked John feeling confident about his new repertoire with agent Stevens.

"Because this is a national security matter you will have no contact with the outside world. That includes family or friends and lawyers," replied Stevens waiting to see John's response.

"How long do you intend to keep me here? Wherever that is, where are we?" asked John his voice now frantic with anxiety at his predicament. Now that he knew more, he was getting more concerned by the minute. He knew the copy of the story about the alien and the coming catastrophe he had sent to his lawyer would be safe. Frank Santoli said think of redundancy measures and he had made two copies. An extra one to insure the story would be told, he had said to himself.

"Perhaps, we should start again?" asked Stevens.

"I have rights."

"You have no rights in here. In fact, because this is a national security matter you are 'persona non grata' with less than zero if that exists," said Stevens.

"Persona no grata…what does that mean exactly?" asked John Cramer.

"At this moment…you don't exist."

"What do you mean?"

"Well, it's like those poor bastards in Guantanamo Bay. They don't have rights either. We treat enemy combatants like we should. Why should they have rights? We feed them and jail them. That's all that matters. They can't harm us in jail. If we need information then they have a choice, it can be easy or hard. It's always up to them if they want to cooperate. Some do and some don't. Now, you have the same choice, you can cooperate or suffer more than you should in here. Now, where did you hide those copies?" asked Stevens his face now had hardened with deep wrinkles on his forehead. Stevens' patience had thinned to the point where his face was turning redder by each minute that passed. He was ready to start knocking Cramer around the room.

"Now, that you have had your food and drink…where did you hide the printed copies?" asked Stevens.

John Cramer replied, "Where am I?"

The next thing John could remember was the force of being hit in the head with a punch. A few slaps around the face and John Cramer was out. The cold water thrown into John's face had had the desired effect. He was quickly willing to answer further questions from the agents.

***

It was now several days since the WR104 protocol had been breached. The three government directors of national security were about to meet at a secure location, close to Washington D.C. The safe house was situated in an abandoned office complex.

Jeremy Katz the Homeland Security director was already sat with his drink waiting for Chandler and Williams to get started with the discussion on events. "I hope you have some good news to report?" said Jeremy Katz.

"Yes. We have identified and arrested a small group of individuals that we believe have been telling the truth. Luckily, for us, the individuals told very few people. We believe from our analysis of data cross referencing that we have all 'persons of interest' that we currently know about. These individuals have been arrested and detained under national security," said David Williams the head of the CIA pausing for a moment to catch his breath before continuing. "There has been no news break about this story and Internet chatter is non-existent. So, we could assume that the individuals we don't have in custody are waiting for the President to break the news, just like we are. Only, we would like the President to forget about informing the world, period."

"What about the reporter from the New York Times has he told us what we want to know?" asked Simon Chandler the National Security director.

Katz interrupting said, "We have to be sure we can hold this story, until, we need to."

"We will have the information about the second copy of the story the reporter wrote and printed soon," said David Williams the CIA director.

"There are using that truth drug, which cannot be fooled," remarked Jeremy Katz who knew most of what went on at the CIA because that was part of Homeland Security's task as a defender of the constitution. It sometimes spied on other security agencies just to make sure the constitution was being upheld to its highest standards.

"That's right; we have given the go-ahead to use the drug on the reporter. It will tie the knot or not," said David Williams.

"What do you mean?" asked Simon Chandler the National Security director sipping his drink and looking for another at the same time.

Much progress had been made since the early days during the Second World War when truth drugs were first used. Chemistry was now leaps and bounds ahead in its ability to construct and synergise any molecule of matter. "I have no doubt my agents will extract the information we want from the reporter. But, there's a problem. We can't be sure that the reporter didn't plan for this to happen. He expects for this drug to be used and so makes plans to deceive us. Now, do you see, it will tie the knot or not," replied Williams as he looked at Chandler and Katz seated likes kings on the gleaming leather couch that aptly supported them without being crowded together at peak times on a busy bus.

"I know how Frank Santoli's mind works. He would have trained them well in the short time he had with them," said Williams.

Chapter 10

Meanwhile, several months had passed and the three government security directors had arranged to meet at the local safe house just outside Washington D.C. The safe house was a former real estate consultancy situated on the ground floor in a quiet cul-de-sac on the outskirts of the capital just off a main highway. The safe house was chosen by the three directors for its easy access to the capital of the United States and because it was relatively secluded, yet within minutes of the capital.

Jeremy Katz the Department of Homeland Security director was first to arrive and was busy pouring himself a tot of Brandy, when Simon Chandler the NSA director walked through the front door.

"I could do with a drink," said Chandler.

"The bar is well stocked," remarked Katz.

"Have you any information on the operation to arrest those individuals we haven't already arrested?" asked Chandler.

"No, I'm waiting to hear what, Williams has to say," replied Katz ready to down another Brandy as David Williams the CIA director walked through the front door.

"I see you two have already started," said Williams

"I needed a drink after the week I've had. My ex wants more money," remarked Katz.

As the three directors sat down around a coffee table to discuss progress and their next moves a mobile phone rang.

"Hello," said David Williams the CIA director on his mobile phone.

"He had posted it to a friend unconnected with this matter," said the voice on the phone.

"Chandler and Katz, we have some new information to discuss," said David Williams.

"Well, gentlemen, we have the news we have been waiting for. The reporter was very clever. He knew we would probably use some sort of truth drug on him, so he had made plans. It turns out; the second copy was in plain sight. Since we last discussed this matter, we have found out where the second copy of the news report that John Cramer had written for publication is. We used a truth drug and it revealed that Cramer had been clever in how to conceal the second copy he had printed. We found out that he had posted the printed copy to himself using the second class postal service."

Katz interrupting said, "Clever bastard."

Williams continuing said, "This was an easy, simple and effective way of hiding the document without a digital footprint. He also burnt the postal receipt for some stamps, so there would be no evidence of where Cramer had scurried the printed copy to. He had allowed for a seven day or more turn around for the letter to be back at his door. Our agents on the initial contact failed to notice Cramer posting the letter during the day of his arrest. So, without the use of the truth drug we would be resorting to other methods to extract the information we required.

Cramer told the agents that he had made a practice run the day he was arrested. He told them he was testing how long the letter would take to go full circle using the second class postal service. The agents had apparently missed Cramer's actions, which only took a second to post during their observation of Cramer that day."

"Are you sure there are no other copies, we have to worry about?" asked Jeremy Katz directing his question at Williams as he sat luxuriously in the leather armchair in the lounge of the real estate office.

"We have checked all Cramer's computers and any devices for their actions. We have also checked all emails and have found no evidence of any other copies, even under a different file name."

"What about key word searches that relate to the story?" asked Chandler eager to get into the conversation and show that he was awake and alert to what was being said.

"Yes, we have done all that and found no evidence that any other copies exist of the story. We are certain we have bottled up the story. What we are not certain of, is how many people he told? We currently have four more people in custody. We are still looking for Frank Santoli, Ahmed Khan, Professor Aaron Mikovitz and Dr. Janet Taylor," replied Williams his demeanour was arrogant at times, especially when he felt confident about a case. Williams continuing said, "I feel confident we can contain the story from reaching the mass media."

"Yes, but what about the others you have failed to capture who could let the cat out the bag," remarked Jeremy Katz.

"Our biggest problem is how we deal with the President. He's still recovering from another dose of the flu. So, he will be up and running in a few days. What's our next move?" replied Williams as he looked at both men sat opposite. He wanted a response with ideas they could discuss. It could be the greatest decision they would ever have to make.

"The President is out biggest challenge. We have to convince him or stop him until it's too late. The sanity of the American way of life depends on what we do. Our decisions will define the future of this great country," said Katz has he glanced at Williams and Chandler expecting both of them would have answers and ideas.

Jeremy Katz was not the type of man who would have creative answers to problems; he relied on others to provide solutions. Katz's motto was don't rock the boat let someone else do it. His career followed a predicable path. He enjoyed his position and status and he wasn't about to lie across the train tracks and wait for his suggestions to come rolling in only to crash and burn. Continuing, he said, "What ideas do you two have?"

"Slow the President down. It's what we have already been doing. We have to make him think that it's his idea. After all his ego likes to be caressed just like any pet. If we can get him to agree with our assessment of the situation then we can extend notification of the public and the world perhaps another six months," responded Williams.

"I agree…slow the President," muttered Chandler, who had had too many shots of brandy.

"We have to be prepared before we can deal with the numbers of people wanting to immigrate to America. We need to set up camps, migration centres, medical facilities and a host of other tasks," stated Katz.

"That's right Katz. A host of other essential tasks, which would have to be in place before the President made the announcement to the world. In fact, we could easily stretch it out for another six months and we have to. Otherwise, America will not be prepared for the social unrest that would follow. I think the President will have to understand for the good of the nation," said Williams.

"Do you think the President will go along with our plans?" asked Chandler.

"If our plans that are presented are not accepted then we will have to remove the President, until, we are ready to bring him back. Flu can last a long time it just depends on his immune system. We should be more concerned with the four fugitives that we have failed to capture. That's our Achilles heel. They could easily spoil our plans. We have to find them and bring them in. Luckily, they have not published what they know. Again, they are probably waiting for the President's announcement. But, its early days…we're on a clock and its ticking and we don't know when it stops. The sooner we find the four fugitives the sooner we can get back in control of the ticking time bomb, which as you know is getting louder as we speak," remarked Williams

"So far, we don't have zilch. Your agents are well trained," said Katz looking at Williams the CIA Director.

"Of course," replied Williams pausing to get a drink from the fridge. He had remembered something Frank Santoli had said to him the last time they had spoken. Continuing he said out loud, "Never make assumptions."

"What do you mean?" asked Katz.

"Yes. What do you mean," repeated Chandler.

Both men were surprised with William's outburst. Williams in their minds was not the sort of person to make out of place statements. They both looked at Williams at first with disbelief, but they both soon realized he was on to something. That something could be the key to catching the four fugitives.

"Never make assumptions…that was what Santoli had said to him years before at a training seminar at the CIA headquarters in Langley, he had remembered. That day Frank Santoli had scored many points ahead of his group. Williams was in that group of a dozen agents being assessed with Frank Santoli and Frank had said that was his secret. "We are making too many assumptions…like Frank said 'Never make assumptions' because the other guys will. Otherwise, we will cross paths and that is how we will catch our prey. We are assuming many things and if Frank is doing the same we will eventually cross paths. The only way is to not make any assumptions on what Frank and his crew are doing or has done," said Williams.

"Plenty of people disappear in Alaska every year," retorted Katz.

"Perhaps he has gone there…who knows where?" said Chandler.

"Our cross referencing and key word mapping on mobile phones, land lines and instant messaging services have been fruitless. Santoli is smart; he would have told them to avoid using names and places associated with this manhunt. He knows what we would be looking for," said Williams.

The cross referencing techniques used by the CIA and other security agencies were sophisticated enough to flag any word associated with key word search terms. This was all done with the help of many different databases and their interoperability between systems allowing for data cross referencing from a host of databases from many different organizations.

Data cross referencing was often referred to as 'data mining' where databases were literally mined for data that matched key search words or terms.

The digitalization of key utilities such as credit cards, phone records, store cards, energy consumption, social platforms and many more organizations made it easier for security agencies to collate data. It was now made possible by the standardization and interoperability of databases around the world. It was now possible to find a 'person of interest' within seconds and not days, weeks and months that it would take for a human investigator to find, if at all. Crutching data was what computers and their software programs were good at. Finding links and matches across dispersed databases and even across the world made catching terrorists a lot easier than tracking their physical movements.

"So, what are your ideas, Williams?" asked Katz.

"Well, we have to stop making assumptions. Frank Santoli is smart, but I think I can out smart him," replied Williams staring into the eyes of Katz. Wondering what Katz was thinking. He knew Katz to be one that never put his own neck on the line. He relied on others to do that. Williams also considered Chandler in the same mould. The only difference was that Chandler was smarter; he would let people know he had an opposite opinion even though he was prepared to go with the flow. "What do you think, Chandler?" asked Williams now staring directly at Chandler waiting for a reply.

"So, what do you suggest?" asked Chandler looking at Williams.

"We continue with our current search terms, but we add the outlier," replied Williams.

"What do you mean?" asked Chandler and Katz.

"The outlier is what I think we have been missing. It catches everyone out in a stock market crash often called the 'black swan' …an event that completely catches the market out. So, the stock market crashes and lots of people lose their money."

"So, what are we missing, Williams?" asked Katz.

"Yes. Tell us, I'm eager to know?" interjected Chandler.

"That's just it, I don't know because I haven't been thinking about it until now," replied Williams.

"Tell us what you do know?" shouted Katz, his patience was running thin.

"It was some time ago and it will take my mind a bit of time to do the research. It was something to do with how to find the unexpected…in our case the outlier. There was a scientific paper written on the subject, which Frank Santoli had praised the virtues of. I will have the information on our next meeting," said Williams.

"What about the other three fugitives?" asked Katz.

"At the moment, we believe that Ahmed Khan is somewhere in Mongolia. We have not seen so far a 'digital footprint' of his movements. So, he is acting the part. He has been well trained by the CIA, which makes our life difficult. We are currently cross checking every lead we get and leaving no stone unturned. We know from the truth drug we used on Cramer the reporter that each member of the group that first made contact with the aliens have no idea on the whereabouts of the other members of the group. It was simple and effective redundancy built in by Frank Santoli in my view," said Williams.

"Sooner or later one of them will make a mistake," chirped Chandler with a confidant smile across his face as if he knew something they didn't.

"Perhaps, you will elaborate on your confidence?" asked Katz.

"The other two, Professor Aaron Mikovitz and Dr. Janet Taylor have not been trained by the CIA. So, I'm expecting either one or both will make a mistake. My guess is you'll find one and the other will not be far away. After all aren't they lovers?" said Chandler sipping his drink after sharing his thoughts.

"Yes, they are lovers," replied Williams.

"But we know all that. You are only stating what we already know, Chandler," said Katz.

"Yes, but you are missing the point. It's easy to see the trees for the forest. Perhaps, we need to concentrate on search terms and criteria related to couples. We know their profiles and head structure, so we should be looking for that on CCTV footage. Okay, we have lots of CCTV footage to crawl through. So look for a match using our sophisticated facial recognition software and leave the leg work for our agents," said Chandler as he laid out his methodology.

"But, aren't our agents already doing this?" asked Katz.

"Yes, in some part, but not like this. Is that right, Williams?" asked Chandler.

"Yes, you are right. But, you're talking about millions of matches to check. We would have to refine the searches using what we do know and then make an educated guess on what they would do next," replied Williams.

"Well, Williams, it's up to you to make some progress. What about the other peripheral players you have locked up, Katz?" asked Chandler as he reached for another drink to quench his thirst.

"We do have some interesting characters locked up. One is a young lad from the observatory in California called Jamie Okeke. He is smart, but he told us everything he knows once we used the truth drug on him. Luckily, for us and the nation, we were able to arrest him before he told his story to the world. The boy is a social platform player. He was just looking for the next story or video to stream to increase his Internet presence in the world of instant media news when we showed up and disrupted his plans," said Katz now in his element. He was in control. It was his department's task the 'Homeland Security Agency' to prevent terror attacks across the United States.

"What about this kid, Jamie Okeke is he a threat to our plans?" asked Williams.

"Currently Jamie Okeke is being held with no contact with the outside world. This guy is a wizard with computers…so we don't have a choice. He's too much of a liability…if he's free and has access to a computer who knows what he could do."

"We have to make sure he doesn't," interjected Chandler.

"Don't worry…the people we have locked up will stay locked up, until, we're ready to release them. We will deal with the legal issues when and if we have to later," said Katz.

***

Professor Aaron Mikovitz's and Dr. Janet Taylor's journey to Frank Santoli's safe house was carefully prepared. Frank had given Aaron and Janet specific instructions of how to proceed. They were to travel by car and meet with Frank at a local landmark in Washington D.C. From there they would follow Frank and drive to the safe house.

Aaron's only concern during the trip was when a car and a bus they were behind on the highway veered too close for comfort and the bus driver had to react quickly to avoid a collision. Janet at the time was sleeping and Aaron didn't see the need to alarm her by informing her they were within a 'hare's breath' of being in a collision with a car.

It had been several months since they had to go into hiding. Frank Santoli had figured that they were safe for now, until, someone made a mistake or the government agencies looking for them got lucky. But, he was worried and so were his comrades. The President hadn't made a speech about the coming catastrophe. What was the President waiting for it was the question everyone in the group was asking, mused Frank as he sat opposite Aaron and Janet in the lounge of his safe house.

"What about Ahmed…is he okay?" asked Aaron.

"Yes. He is fine and not able to travel here. He is ready and able to carry out any actions we decide here, today. Don't forget what I taught you about redundancy. He is there when we need him."

"Frank, don't you think it was a big risk arranging this meeting here?" asked Janet.

"I had no choice…it was safer for you and me…for you to come here. It makes sense…a young couple in disguise, rather than me alone. Besides, you have a car that is registered to another couple within the same age range. The car I used to get here is hidden away in the garage. I've been using the bus to get my groceries," replied Frank.

"Well, let's get down to business," said Aaron.

"Yes," agreed Janet.

"We have all been asking the same question…why the President hasn't made any announcements. It's been more than three months, since we went into hiding. So, do we break our silence and announce to the world what we know. And hope the world takes notice and doesn't label us as some crack pots who have smoked too much weed," said Frank as he tried to make light of the situation with a chuckle and a laugh.

"Perhaps, the whole world will need to be smoking pot by the years to come," said Aaron.

"Let's be serious, we have to decide now," retorted Janet.

"I vote to wait for the President, because we have no guarantee what we have to say will persuade anyone. We will just end up locked up in jail. Remember, those that are currently locked up have had no contact with the outside world," said Frank Santoli.

"I vote the same, Frank. It's better to wait," said Aaron.

I agree," repeated Janet.

"So, we're all agreed we shall wait until the President makes an announcement. If the President hasn't made an announcement in the next three months then we will have to take action," said Frank.

"Do you think we can stay hidden from the authorities for another three months, Frank," asked Janet.

"Don't see a reason why not. As long as we all keep doing what we have be doing and not make any stupid mistakes…like start using a credit card," replied Frank.

"Perhaps, we should seek another meeting with the President?" asked Aaron.

"Just how do we do that, without being arrested first?" asked Janet.

"Yes, you are right Aaron. I would like another meeting with the President, but the risks are high. But, sooner or later, we may have no choice to act regardless of the consequences," replied Frank.

***

Within a few days of the meeting with Professor Aaron Mikovitz and Dr. Janet Taylor, Frank Santoli was on the move again and relocating to new secure safe house. Now that Aaron and Janet knew where his original safe house was Frank considered it was prudent to move. Frank had considered that if Aaron and Janet were captured then they could only reveal his original safe house. He had also thought his original bolt hole was too close to the centre of power and a likely starting point for the authorities in Washington D.C to search first. Frank's training had convinced him of the need to move far away from the clutches of the government agencies that were trying to find him from the centre of government in Washington D.C.

It was a chilly morning in Washington D.C. as the winter had just started when Frank boarded a bus going south to a warmer climate. He had decided to head for Louisiana where he figured he had an ideal safe house. The safe house was a log cabin in the depths of the swamp area and the nearest town many miles away. When Frank arrived in Louisiana it had taken several bus journeys to get there and now the longest part of the journey to the safe house would begin by boat.

The log cabin was situated on land that was surrounded by swamps and submerged forest. The cabin had been owned by Frank's father and never mentioned in any legal document. Frank's father had said that he would get around to legalizing the transaction, but he never did because he had won the log cabin and the land it sits on in a poker game. He preferred to hold the land and the cabin until it was won back at some future date. But, it never did change hands again. So, Frank inherited the log cabin and the land after his father had passed away only a few years past. He had meant to inform the land registry and legalize the property, but since his father's death he had not found the time to do so. Frank had been to the cabin many times as a child and he had fond memories of the times he had spent there with his father. It was an ideal safe house, he said to himself.

Frank loaded the boat with some essential supplies of food and diesel and headed out into the swamp. The boat used a single outboard motor and had been well looked after by Frank's father who used the vessel to get in and out of the swamp.

"Thanks for the help," said Frank to the local man he called a friend who had kept an eye on the boat moored next to his own boat deep in the back woods of the swamps of Louisiana.

"If you need any help, let me know," said Jake the local man who had a deep southern accent and lived in a log cabin much like the cabin Frank was about to live in. But, it would be totally off the grid, without electricity or any mobile phone signal. If he needed to use the mobile phone he would have to travel back to Jake's the local man's cabin or the nearest town. Jake had said that on a good day he could get a mobile phone signal, but it was understood that he was most likely on the outer limits of any mobile phone tower transmitting and receiving a signal in the area.

As Frank travelled down into the swamp he followed the course you knew well. It was only three years since the last time he had visited the cabin, but much had changed. The forest of trees had grown in some parts of the swamp, but there were local landmarks that Frank could follow. On the journey, he thought about Iron Smart the alien and what the alien had warned about. It would be a complete tragedy if places like this swamp with its flora and wildlife were to disappear because in the future the land was needed for the increasing population and would be drained and cultivated for crops.

Frank could smell the swamp water and hear some yellow-crown night herons squawking and then saw them circling low in the sky above the mist. The bird sounds mixed in with the hum of the outboard motor was all he heard as he continued his journey into the swamp. It was close to mid-day as the heat of the winter sun had started to clear the low mist above the swamp water.

As Frank moved the boat in and out of the submerged forest and after carefully avoiding any fallen trees he knew he was only a couple of hours away from the log cabin. He would arrive at the cabin before it got dark. He wasn't about to risk travelling in the boat at night. His father had said many times that the alligators were more active at night and that was precisely why he wanted to be on dry land before dark fall.

"And there it is," he said out loud.

It was the wreck of an old metal fishing boat that straddled the swamp and dry land that Frank had been looking for. It had been three years since the last time he had seen the wreck. The rusting wreck had been a landmark for many years and had helped him and his father navigate the path to the log cabin on numerous occasions. As Frank passed the fishing boat he wondered for a few moments on how the fishing boat finished its life. He was surprised nobody had claimed it and salvaged the vessel for scrap. Perhaps, it was too expensive to salvage and not worth the time and cost in scrap metal, he mused.

After an hour had passed, Frank could see the log cabin come into view. The log cabin was surrounded by forest on land that had never been swamped by water. The trees were far enough away from the cabin that they didn't pose a threat in a storm from falling over. He could see the small wooden jetty that he and his father had built many years before to anchor his boat in the swamp. His first impressions of the log cabin from a distance were good. Jake had replaced a few wooden shingles on the roof of the cabin over the years after a storm, but apart from that the cabin looked in good repair. Jake had kept an eye on the log cabin over the years and he had done a good job, he said to himself.

After unloading his essential supplies onto the jetty he made his way to the log cabin. He had enough supplies to last for weeks. He had already made up his mind that he would survive mostly on what food he could kill or catch in the swamp. The key to the door of the cabin had been carefully hidden behind a stack of firewood drying out under the overhanging roof.

As Frank opened the door of the cabin he could smell the place hadn't been used for a while. A deep over-powering smell of musk filled his nostrils and reminded him of the time when he had searched an abandoned apartment block for evidence in a crime. The apartment block was damp from the rain that had leaked in over a period of time and wrecked each apartment. He decided to light the wood stove and air out the log cabin and prepare for the evening with some hot food.

Opening the shutters to the only window that looked out towards the swamp and the jetty, he noticed in the distance the outline of two people in a fishing boat pass by. He consoled himself that he wasn't the only soul that frequented this part of the swamp, but he surmised that the log cabin would be an ideal safe house, at least for now, he said to himself.

The main problem for Frank was that he was now totally cut off from his fellow comrades, but not from the world because he had a small battery radio, which would pick up any local radio broadcasts. Frank knew that the range of mobile phone towers were limited to a few miles compared to radio broadcasts that often spanned continents.

He would listen out for any news from the President and if need be make contact with his comrades. If he had to make contact with his comrades then the only way he could was to make the journey to Jake's home or somewhere nearby where he could hopefully get a signal for his mobile phone. Frank knew that Jake had a small generator that he used to power some of the tools he used and surmised that Jake also recharged his mobile phone this way.

The only 'Achilles heel' was the communication data between mobile phones, he said to himself. If you knew about one end of the contact between mobile phones then you could work out which cell tower was used and from that home in on the area and narrow the search. In the digital age, it was easy to cross check data from cell towers and workout the whereabouts of individual users.

***

It was early one morning, when Frank was chopping some wood for the stove when he heard the nearby brush crackle, as if someone or something was approaching the cabin. From the noise that he heard and the direction it was coming from, he surmised, it was possibly a bear or a deer. He didn't think it would be a person because from that direction the forest was impassable with much of it submerged by the swamp. You would have needed a boat to traverse the forest, he said to himself. As the noise got louder, he caught the first glimpse of the outline of a human form appear from the edge of the forest. At this point, his training as a CIA agent had taught him to think first before taking action. His gun was inside the cabin and he wasn't prepared to kill a government agent just because they had found him, unless, he was forced to, he said to himself. Still clasping the hatchet in one hand, and using the other to shade his eyes from the sun, he called out to the person.

Frank cried out, "Hello, can I help you?"

Frank shouted again, hoping for a favourable response, "Hello, who is it?"

The human figure was only a few feet away, but Frank struggled to see the person against the back drop of the dark forest and the early morning sun blinding his view.

"I am Iron Smart, we have met before," said the metallic voice from the edge of the forest that sounded like a tin can ringing.

As the alien approached closer, Frank could see the alien he had met before. But, Frank had noticed that the alien had changed color since the last time they had met. The alien was mostly black in color compared to the silvery color it had before. Its skin, if you could call it skin was more like what the knights in medieval-ages wore into battle. Frank surmised, the alien probable had the ability to change color at will, it was something he could do with at times, he said to himself. There were parts of the alien's skin that had reflected the light like sunlight that dazzles and sparkles on a calm sea, which had blurred his view.

"What do you want?" asked Frank as he lay down the axe on the ground figuring that if the alien wanted to harm him then it would have far superior weapons it could use. He continued and said, "Didn't you say you were leaving for your home planet?"

"Why hasn't your President informed the world about the cosmic rays?" asked Iron Smart with its monotone voice, which made each word have a metallic ring and a slight echo like it was bouncing about within a mountain range.

"Perhaps, you should ask him, not me. Why would I know what the President is thinking," replied Frank

"You are the leader of the group who came aboard our spacecraft and you must help," said Iron Smart.

"You could land outside the White House and ask the President to act now," said Frank rhetorically. He wasn't expecting an answer and for a minute forgot he was communicating with an alien. What Jake would think if he saw me now, he said to himself.

"I made an agreement with your President that we would not land at the White House," said Iron Smart.

"Okay, what do you want me to do?" asked Frank.

"We want your President to inform the world before it's too late. We stayed in your solar system. We could then monitor the progress." replied Iron Smart.

"How did you find me?" asked Frank who was intrigued to find out how easy or not it was to find him. He had assumed that he had covered all the bases, and the government agencies looking for him had had no joy.

"When you entered our spacecraft our technology immediately scanned your body for its unique biometric rhythm. The particles in your body that you call atoms make a rhythm that is constantly vibrating at a certain frequency. This frequency can then be multiplied and tracked by our technology. I told you about viewing the universe as a liquid. All atoms are moving. Everything from rocks to people, they always emit a frequency," replied Iron Smart.

"So, you want me to inform the President of this meeting and convince him to tell the world about the cosmic rays that are about to hit the Earth?" said Frank.

"Yes, or we will land outside the White House," stated Iron Smart.

"How much time do I have before you will land outside the White House?" asked Frank.

"In your time you have seven days from first light tomorrow."

"Why are you so interested in saving our planet?"

"Life is everywhere in the universe. Intelligent life is not."

"Okay, I will try to inform the President one way or another. If I fail then you will have to land outside the White House and inform the world in seven days' time." said Frank who knew now that his mission could not fail. The world would know the facts regardless of whether he failed or not. He had several options in mind before this visit by the alien; it was only his future discussion with Aaron and Janet that would finalise the plan.

"I will leave you now," said Iron Smart.

Frank watched the alien turn and walk back into the forest and within seconds the shape of the alien soon disappeared into the darkness. Frank thoughts immediately turned to what he had to do. He quickly gathered what he needed especially his mobile phone and headed towards the jetty. It was still early morning as he steered his boat out into the swamp towards Jake's home.

Passing the landmark of the rusting fishing boat Frank steered his boat into the nearby river. He noticed the numerous alligators on the shore line almost lifeless as if they were all sun bathing. The alligators didn't have a care in the world, he thought. His thoughts turned to the plan he had in mind. He had already worked out the route and where he needed to be at a certain time.

***

It had been over three months since Frank Santoli and the other members of the group had visited the President at the White House and had listened to the alien Iron Smart warn about the coming apocalypse. Every day since then, Frank had listened to his battery radio for news from the President. There had been no announcement about the coming catastrophe. He had begun to get worried why the President hadn't made an announcement? He also had made an agreement with Aaron and Janet that they would wait for another three months before taking action. The world had to know what was about to happen, he said to himself.

Over the last three months living quietly surrounded by swamps, he had considered the options. Each day that passed he went over the options in his mind, carefully analyzing the 'pros and cons' of each option. He wondered, what Aaron and Janet would say. The three of them would have to meet somewhere safe and discuss the action they were prepared to take. Aaron had said they were living in California, but not where. Frank had considered it best to meet halfway between Louisiana and California, but it had to be safe. He surmised that the government agencies looking for them would have increased their efforts to find them. That morning when he set off with his mobile phone, he was hoping he could get a signal at Jake's place and not have to travel to the nearest town.

He had a place in mind to meet Aaron and Janet when he docked his boat at the small wooden jetty near Jake's log cabin. But, he had changed his mind about meeting Aaron and Janet halfway because of the risks. Frank had considered the risk too great, especially after the last time they had met. He had all the training, and so it was up to him to get to Aaron. He had noticed that Jake was likely home by seeing his vehicle parked in its usual spot and that also his boat was tied to the jetty. Unless, he was out in the forest hunting for game, he surmised. He was right; there was no sign of Jake. Switching on his mobile, he noticed the tentative signs that the mobile phone was trying to make a 'handshake' with a nearby mobile phone tower by the sound it was making.

Frank cried out, hoping his friend would hear him, "Hello, Jake, are you there?" It wasn't polite in Louisiana, deep in the swamp territory just to knock on their door and announce your presence. He was aware that many people could be spooked by this action. He called out again, but there was no answer. He also looked through the only window of the log cabin, but there was no sign of life. He then sat in the rocking chair on the porch and tried again his mobile phone for a signal. This time the phone was dialling Aaron's phone number with success.

"Hello, it's me, we need to meet," said Frank, who had told Aaron and the rest of the group not to mention any names while on the phone. He had told them previously that the government agencies looking for them would employ sophisticated communication tracking technology and be able to cross check names and identify likely candidates for further scrutiny.

"Hi, it's been awhile," said Aaron, who knew it was Frank on the phone by his New York accent and the fact that no one else had the number to his new phone.

"I have decided to come to you. I will meet with you and your partner at your favourite location on Friday this week at mid-day. I have some options that we need to discuss. In the meantime, good hunting."

Just as Frank ended the call the mobile phone connection disconnected as he had begun to reflect on the call.

Aaron knew immediately where the meeting would take place from a previous conservation he had had with Frank the last time they had met. The extra information of 'good hunting' confirmed where the meeting would take place. Frank was no fool and Aaron was beginning to like the way Frank operated. Frank didn't over elaborate, he just kept things as simple as he could, and he was his kind of spook, he said to himself.

"Hello Jake, been waiting for you to return."

"Hello Frank...it's been a few weeks since I saw you last," replied Jake pausing to put a large lung fish he had caught in the swamp on the table he used to prepare the fish to cook.

"It's a good catch, Jake."

"Yes, why don't you stay for lunch and have a beer with me?" asked Jake.

"Sounds like the best offer I've had today," replied Frank who wasn't worried about the time. He had calculated the distance from Louisiana to California and knew he had plenty of time to make the meeting with Aaron and Janet. He was planning to make the trip on Wednesday leaving plenty of time should any snags occur. Tomorrow, he would leave the log cabin early and make his way by bus to California.

"Tomorrow, I will leave my boat tied by your jetty. I'm going away for few days. I will see you when I get back, Jake."

"No problem, Frank. You know, I've always looked after the boat when your father was away."

Frank knew that Jake wasn't the type of guy who would ask questions. And if he did then Frank could easily tell him a lie and give him a story. He realised long ago when he was a young boy with his father exploring for the first time the swamps that Jake had honesty you could trust. Jake would often give his advice freely and honestly when his father asked. They were like different ends of a spectrum. His father had been raised in the city and Jake was raised in the swamps of Louisiana. But, they had become good friends over the years despite the culture gap.

"Get the log burner going, Frank, were cooking that fish I caught, this morning," said Jake as he flayed the fish before cooking.

"That looks and smells great. What did you do?" asked Frank.

"I used a little southern sauce to spice it up a bit," replied Jake with a wry smile like a child with a secret to share.

"I saw some strange lights in the sky around here the other night. Did you see them?" asked Jake.

Frank at first was stunned by the question. But, he knew the answer and wasn't about to tell Jake. "Most of the time at night I'm sleeping after a hard day catching and hunting for food."

"Looks like the food is ready," said Jake.

"Let's eat."

"I must tell you this story," said Jake.

"It's about thirty years ago now. I was in my boat looking for suitable places to set traps for alligators, down near the fishing boat that is beached on the edge of the swamp. You know the one? Near Devils Pass, where the river forks to the left and to the right of the old fishing boat."

"Yes, I know the one that's just rusting away and hasn't been claimed for salvage by anyone," replied Frank.

"Yes, that is strange, especially, when the price of scrap these days is high."

"In the clear blue sky more or less above me was an UFO that was about three hundred feet in the air. It wasn't making any kind of sound, it just hovered in the sky for about five minutes, before accelerating at what seemed an incredible speed vertically into the clouds and into space, I guess. At the time it frightened the shit out of me," said Jake with a chuckle in his tone of voice.

"It would scare anyone confronted with that scenario," said Frank pausing before continuing. "Are you trying to relate these lights you saw the other night to this UFO experience you had as a teenager?" asked Frank.

"Yes, I believe both were UFOs. And it's not just me. Many of the folk around here have had similar experiences over the years. If they come for me, then I've got my shotgun ready and waiting," said Jake with a tone of voice that worried Frank.

"Don't worry Jake. It's no good worrying about something you have no control over," said Frank.

"I guess, you are right, Frank."

"Listen! Jake," Frank said in a commanding tone of voice and repeated what he had said earlier. "It's no good worrying about something you have no control over. Keep that in mind and you will sleep better at night."

"Okay, let's have some beers before you have to leave. You don't want to be going back to your cabin in the night with all those alligators looking for food," said Jake with wide grin across his face and a slight chuckle in his voice.

Frank knew that alligators were mainly active at night when it got cooler. During the day alligators would spend most of their time warming their bodies in the sun and avoiding any excursion during the heat of the day, which was the best time to explore the swamps and to get back to the log cabin. Frank wasn't worried because over the past weeks he had made several trips back and forth getting supplies, so now he was getting to know his way through the swamp.

***

Early the next morning, Frank set off into the swamps again and steered the boat towards Jake's home again. Jake had promised him a ride to town in his truck.

As Frank tied his boat to Jake's jetty, he could see that Jake was already waiting for him.

Frank cried out, "Morning, Jake."

"It's another good day," said Jake, as he rose from his rocking chair on the porch. He continued, "I'm ready when you are."

The drive to the town was only about eight miles. Frank had little time for small talk. And Jake wasn't the type of person to ask questions, so Frank stayed silent for much of the way.

Entering the town, Frank thanked Jake for the ride and waited by the bus stop for a bus into New Orleans, which was a major bus terminal for connecting routes to much of America. From there he had found out previously that there would be two bus changes before he arrived in California and that he would arrive by travelling overnight early the next day.

It had been a comfortable bus ride for Frank, until, he saw a young man stealing from another passenger who happened to be asleep while the crime took place. For a moment, he was ready to act when the bus driver confronted the man and handled the situation. Frank saw the thief try to bully the bus driver, but Frank refrained from taking action. He didn't want to blow his cover. He would have had to possibly make out a police form as a witness. He told the police that he didn't see anything because he was asleep when the fracas occurred. He didn't like bullies from his days at school and living with two older brothers. But, he had other issues on his mind more important to consider.

***

When Frank Santoli arrived at the hunting lodge in the Joshua Tree National Park, California, he could see that Aaron and Janet had already arrived. It would be just the three of them to make the decisions. But, events had already played their hand with the unexpected visit of Iron Smart at Frank's hideout in the swamp. Frank explained to Aaron and Janet the visit by the alien at the cabin and what its demands were.

"So, the visit of the alien has already played our hand. We have no choice, but, to go ahead and do what it says," said Aaron.

"We have to go ahead with what the alien wants," chirped Janet like a singing bird just ready and waiting to tweet. It was Janet's way, she was precocious as ever.

"Yes, we have only a few days to inform the President or they will land on the lawn of the White House. The world will know one way or another. Iron Smart was specific on the time. I don't think the world can handle the existence of aliens and at the same time the potential destruction of the planet," remarked Frank.

"So, what do we do?" asked Aaron who was perplexed at what to do.

"Yes, what can we do?" asked Janet rhetorically.

"I have a plan, which can be put into action within a few hours," replied Frank with a commanding tone of voice.

"What is your plan?" asked Aaron.

Frank explained to Aaron and Janet that he had a contact in the White House. The secret contact would pass a message to the President without anyone being aware. The message would be encrypted from end to end and only my contact would be able to decipher. The message would then be secretly passed to the President with the details of what Iron Smart wanted to happen.

"It sounds like you have everything covered?" asked Aaron.

Janet found the words; she had wanted to say from the beginning of the saga, "It's down to Iron Smart to save the day."

"I hope it works?" piped Aaron with some doubt in his tone of voice that was clearly audible to Frank and Janet.

"And there's something else. Iron Smart said that there was a chance the planet could be saved. The alien outlined a plan to save the planet by using the gravitational force of its mother ship. The spacecraft would beam out this gravitational force and force the cosmic rays around the force field similar to how our planet's magnetic force directs harmful radiation from the Sun away from the Earth."

"Wow! You know more?" asked Janet rhetorically.

"A mother ship, shit. Where's that been hiding?" asked Aaron.

"I don't know? But, my guess is the dark side of the Moon," replied Frank.

"Shit…the aliens are everywhere," chirped Janet like a Jack out of the box.

"The important thing is, they are willing to help the world," explained Frank.

"I hope it works…or we are fried," stated Janet.

"Do you think it has a chance, Aaron?" asked Frank.

"From what you say, I don't know? It depends on a lot of factors that I don't know? Like how big is the energy of the force field? How big is the mother ship?" replied Aaron.

"If Iron Smart says there is a chance then, we have to believe that. But, the question is, why are they helping us?" asked Janet who wanted answers to questions both Frank and Aaron were already thinking the same.

"Like they said before, intelligent life is rare," replied Frank.

"I hope you are right, Frank, otherwise, we're cooked," stated Janet.

"So, we are in agreement, we send the message to the President?" asked Frank.

"Yes, we have no other choice," announced Janet with a commanding tone of voice that shocked both Frank and Aaron at the same time.

"What are your thoughts, Aaron?" asked Frank who was keen to know what Aaron thought of the alien's idea to save the planet.

Aaron was deep in thought. "I guess, we have no other choice," said Aaron.

"I will send the message, today. And for safety at some point on my journey back," responded Frank.

Aaron explained to Janet and Frank what he thought of Iron Smart's plan to save the planet from the harmful cosmic rays. He explained that the force field would only have to be wide enough to deflect the cosmic rays from Earth. Aaron explained that even though the cosmic gamma rays would be as wide as the solar system the force field from the alien mother ship would only need to protect Earth. The rest of the solar system would not be protected and if life existed there then it would have to start again. The energy needed to protect a mother ship from missiles and other projectiles he explained could protect our planet. He explained that the energy needed to protect from these missiles and other projectiles must be substantial.

Henceforth, the force field would deflect the cosmic gamma rays from the planet. Aaron explained that he would have to make some calculations, but the logic was sound. If a force field can stop a missile then it could be just enough to stop the energetic particles of the cosmic gamma rays.

"So, you think it can work, Aaron?" asked Frank.

"Yes, it's got a good chance and the only one we have."

"So, we go back into hiding, until the President makes an announcement?" asked Janet.

"Yes, I will send the message and then we wait," replied Frank.

"Perhaps, by the end of next week we can come out of hiding," said Aaron.

Frank explained to Aaron and Janet that they were still fugitives and they may have to stay hidden for longer. He explained what some of the security implications were regarding their disappearance from the government agencies. Frank explained that the agencies tracking them were not likely to forget that they had been fugitives on the run. The government agencies would want a full brief on what we were doing. How we evaded them. What we did to foil there attempts to find us. Frank explained the agencies would improve their techniques from our experience. He explained that the government could want to keep us quiet.

"We know too much and certain powers may not like that," said Frank.

"Well, we will have to take a chance at some point. Because I would like to get back to living some sort of normal life," said Aaron.

***

It had been over three months since the alien Iron Smart had met with the President at the White House and warned of the coming apocalypse. As far as David Williams the head of the CIA and his other two accomplices Simon Chandler and Jeremy Katz were concerned they had prevented the President from making an announcement to the world about the coming apocalypse up until now. It was now up to the President to announce to the world what was about to happen to the world and what plans they had to save the world from this catastrophe.

"I know now how Damocles must have felt with that sword tangling above his head by just one single hair from a horse's tail. Power for just one day is enough for most people with the sword the great leveller of responsibility," said the President.

The President surveyed the room. He noticed that most of his cabinet were present. He remained silent for few moments considering his thoughts. The President felt the same as the Greek King Dionysius who was right to place the sword above Damocles head tangling by a single hair. It showed that Damocles was envious of the king's power, but also how precarious the king's power was tangling on a cliff edge at any time.

"Are we ready with our forward planning?" asked the President.

"Yes, we have everything in hand. The last three months we have been busy with our nearest neighbours and we have agreed the terms of how we will handle the influx of refugees," said Jeremy Katz head of Homeland Security and responsible for the stability of the United States of America.

"We are aware that most of the world already knows a major event is about to befall our world. The Internet has been rife with stories and conspiracies for months that something major was about to happen," said David Williams.

"Where have these stories come from?" asked the President.

"Most likely from our allies, we had to inform the governments of our nearest neighbours so that we could arrange terms on how to deal with such a catastrophe," said Simon Chandler the head of the NSA.

"That's right," agreed Jeremy Katz.

"Why did we wait and not inform the whole world from the beginning?" asked Dr. Phoebe Gupta special advisor to the President.

Most people at the President's meeting were unfamiliar with the presence of Dr. Phoebe Gupta. At the beginning of the cosmic ray saga the President had appointed the astrophysicist to act as special advisor to the President and its cabinet. Phoebe Gupta was born in Seattle, Washington State to parents who had emigrated from Mumbai, India, shortly after the Second World War. Phoebe attended Washington State University gaining a first in astrophysics. She was now in her forties and never previously married, although she had come close to marrying on one other occasion. Although, her parents were found of introducing her to potential candidates, she preferred her own judgement even if that meant disappointing her well-meaning parents. With jet black hair the color of night and deep brown eyes that caught the attention of many beholders and an olive skin, she had inherited the facial characteristics of her parent's birthplace.

"Perhaps, we should have, but there's no point in putting out the fire by being set a light," snapped Jeremy Katz before continuing. "We had to make sure our plans to host an influx of refugees were sound and ready to go."

"What are our plans to host these refugees?" asked the President.

"We have set up camps all across America where we can initially house these refugees. These camps will serve as new cities where the refugees will be initially medically checked and allocated jobs across America," replied Simon Chandler who had devised the plans for housing the refugees.

"Do we have a number on how many refugees will come to America?" asked the President.

"We have divided up the numbers between us and the countries participating in saving the world and the number could be anywhere between 100 and 200 million," replied David Williams.

"Wow! We will be almost doubling our population," gasped the President.

"It may end up doubling, if some of our allies don't play ball," responded Jeremy.

"Yes, this could happen, but we have planned for such a scenario," said David Williams.

"What plans have you made, David?" asked the President.

"We will create more habitable land to house these refugees and in fifty to hundred years most of these people or their descendants will be able to return to their native countries," replied David Williams.

"Is that true?" asked the President.

"Yes, most areas in the kill zone will be habitable within that sort of time frame. It could be even a shorter time frame. It wasn't long after the Chernobyl nuclear accident in nineteen eighty six in the state of Ukraine that some of the wildlife in the effective area started to return," replied David Williams.

"Yes, but what we face in less than eighteen months is on a magnitude much more destructive," said Jeremy Katz eager to promote himself within the cabinet in front of the President.

"Yes, you are right, Jeremy, but let's hear what Dr. Gupta has to say on the matter," interjected the President who had promoted Dr. Phoebe Gupta as a special advisor to the cabinet and the President.

"As you already know my background is in nuclear physics and radiation, I will begin with a summary of the effects of this catastrophe," replied Dr. Phoebe Gupta.

"First, you are both right," Dr. Gupta said as she looked at David Williams and Jeremy Katz in turn before continuing her assessment of the coming catastrophe.

Dr. Phoebe Gupta went on to explain what she and other leading nuclear scientists thought would be the most likely effects of the cosmic gamma rays.

The accident at Chernobyl, Ukraine in April, 1986 was the first time a nuclear reactor had exploded in the history of nuclear power generation. The accident at Chernobyl was far worse than the accidents at Three Mile Island in America and the Fukushima Daiichi nuclear power plant in Japan, because of the amount of radiation fall out that was dispersed over a wider area. And because of prevailing winds the radiation from the disaster at Chernobyl was spread across much of Europe. The highly radiative particles were blown high into the atmosphere from the explosion at the nuclear power plant in Chernobyl, which made the accident a lot more dangerous for grazing animals and the humans consuming any milk or meat. Because these radiative particles and dust went high into the atmosphere they were able to reach much of Europe by means of the planet's rotation.

"Why are these cosmic rays more dangerous than the accident at Chernobyl?" asked the President who hadn't had time to read the doctor's report and was beginning to become anxious about the speech he had prepared for the world.

"It's all about speed and dosage," replied Dr. Gupta who had noticed from the look on the face of the President that he was beginning to look more worried by the minute. She saw that the deep lines of wrinkles on his forehead were more prominent amongst the golden tan the President was sporting, since his short holiday in Florida.

"Perhaps, you can speed up your summary, Dr. Gupta," interjected David Williams who was not the sort of man who worried about etiquette. He had grown used to the power and the prestige that being the head of the CIA had given him. With this power and prestige came the feeling of superiority over most people even at times the President.

"Please, continue, Dr. Gupta and don't worry about David. He has a habit of trying to steer things his way," said the President.

"Yes, thank you Mr. President. I will continue and do my best to speed up," said Dr Gupta as she paused to witness the reaction of David Williams' face before continuing her summary with a wry smile across her lips, which she allowed to linger so that everyone gathered in the Oval Office could see. "The cosmic gamma rays will be travelling at close to the speed of light and will have the ability to strip the electrons from the atoms that make up every living thing."

As Dr. Gupta continued with her summary, she explained that the radiation dosage would be significantly higher then what was experienced in the disaster at Chernobyl. We receive radiation every day from the sun, but most of the deadly forms of radiation from the sun are deflected by our planet's magnetic field. We can see the effects of this radiation as the particles interact with our atmosphere and are channelled vertically down at the poles of the earth's magnetic field. In the northern hemisphere we call this light show the 'Aurora Borealis' or the northern lights and the 'Aurora Australis' are the lights seen at the South Pole.

Dr. Gupta went on to explain that, we already live with background radiation, but because it's in such a low dosage it has no material effect on humans or animals. Although, she did say there was an anomaly in man's evolution, which she couldn't explain why or indeed other scientists couldn't either. She went on to explain that scientists were currently mystified as to why over the course of millions of years of man's evolution that we hadn't developed and produced proteins in our DNA to protect us from the harmful effects of radiation. She contrasted man's evolution with the recent studies of the flora and fauna surrounding the disaster at Chernobyl.

Recent studies had shown that some species of birds that are common to the Chernobyl area had over successive generations and the course of the last thirty or more years had changed their DNA enabling them to produce anti-radiation proteins called codon-anti-codon. These proteins and their ability to combat the harmful effects of radiation have given the scientific community hope that in the near future these proteins could be introduced into the DNA of mankind.

"So, there is hope for mankind in the near future," interjected the President who was now beginning to smile as if a large weight had lifted from his shoulders. He now felt the worry of the world fade away like snow melting under the rays of the sun.

"Yes, Mr. President there is hope that the coming catastrophe can be mitigated over the years," replied Dr Gupta pausing to stand up and show the cabinet and the President using a white board how this could be done.

Dr Gupta showed an example on the white board how the anti-radiation proteins could be introduced into the DNA of Homo sapiens. She explained that radiation spikes had caused mutations to occur in the past and it was understood that these mutations had contributed to the rapid diversity in plant and animal life. The fossil record is proof that after mass extinctions that the earth had experienced, we can see an abundance of life, she reiterated. It was no coincidence she emphasised that this was the case, and that through careful planning and management it would be possible for people to return home to their countries.

"How long would it take for that to happen?" asked the President who was now eager to participate, now that he knew there was hope for mankind? He was glad that he had assigned Dr. Gupta as a special advisor after he had consulted with his cabinet. The fact that the doctor was an authority on nuclear science and was well respected by her peers was enough to convince him of her need.

"It could take anywhere between twenty and a hundred years," replied Dr. Gupta.

"Why can't you be more specific on the time?" asked the President.

"There have been no long term studies on the issue. So, I cannot be precise on the time it would take for the environment to recover and our ability to deal with the radiation," replied Dr. Gupta pausing to show a graph on the white board that was the shape of a bell curve. Continuing she said, "This graph shows the many different animals including mankind and the levels of radiation we think they can cope with. You can see there are a few outliers, but most of the species are well within the bell. This you would expect from a bell curve. After all, we evolved at the same time and place. But, it's the few outliers on the edges of the bell curve that pose the most questions and mysteries."

"What do you mean, doctor," asked David Williams who was most intrigued. He hadn't had the time to read Dr. Gupta's report, but was listening to every word that came from the lips of the doctor. He always said to his friends that it was better to ask a question then continue in the dark. He wasn't worried by what other people were thinking. He had learnt to ask questions at university and not to worry what other students were thinking.

"We don't fully understand why the beetle can withstand many times the radiation that mankind can or why some species of bird can produce proteins that protect them from harmful radiation," replied Dr. Gupta who had noticed the change in manner from the CIA chief. Continuing she said, "These questions and more are what are being studied right now. Perhaps, in a few years we will know more and be able to make the link that solves these anomalies and mysteries."

The doctor went on to explain that although the city of Chernobyl has been desolate since the time of the nuclear accident there exists today many people who continue to live on the outskirts of the city. These people were mostly poor subsistence farmers who have lived in the area all their lives and refuse to move elsewhere. Admittedly, these people were old the doctor explained, but had shown no harmful side effects from the radiation fallout. She explained that the old people were consuming what they grew and reared on their land.

"Why are these people not suffering from the radiation?" asked Jeremy Katz who had recently suffered the death of his father from cancer. The tone of his voice echoed an anger that he tried to hide. But, the colleagues that really knew him knew he was trying to hide his grief.

"With radiation it's all about the dosage. And cancer can take a long time to manifest its self. And it also depends on many other factors such as each individual's metabolism. And the ability of our body's immune system to destroy cancer cells," replied Dr. Gupta pausing for moment and gaining the attention of the cabinet and the President before closing her summary. "Looking on the bright side for just for a moment, I feel we can look to a brighter future. Well, that concludes my summary of my report are there any questions?"

"Yes, you mentioned there are some anomalies with why some animals and organisms have the ability to cope with radiation and others don't. Can you explain why this should be?" asked Jeremy Katz who was wondering if the cancer his father died from was a genetic problem or something else.

"That is a good question. Well, from the bell curve we can see that the data doesn't lie. And there are anomalies, which shouldn't be there if you consider how Darwin's theory of evolution works. But, I'm not a biologist and therefor my answer is only an educated guess. It would seem to be genetic," replied Dr. Gupta.

"Are there any other questions for Dr. Gupta?" asked the President pausing for a moment before continuing, "No…good then I thank, Dr Gupta, for her summary. I will now ask the Secretary of State to give us an update on plans to safeguard the flora and fauna of the affected areas."

The Secretary of State was a large and well-rounded middle-aged man who was a former Harvard law graduate and army officer. He had been promoted to the post as Secretary of State by the President after serving several years as a Director of the CIA.

"Thank you, Mr President," said Dominic Penn the Secretary of State as he ruffled some papers in his hands. He had decided not to stand up due to an injury to his lower back he had sustained in a tank that he was commanding during the last Iraqi war. Reaching for his eye glasses that he wore only when he had to read documents, he continued with the update. "As you all know, we have less than eighteen months before the world will be turned upside down. Over the past few months since the alien Iron Smart informed us of the coming catastrophe, we have been coordinating plans to form an Ark of sorts to save as much of the flora and fauna in the affected areas. We are now ready and waiting for the go ahead to put those plans into action."

"What kind of Ark do you have in mind?" asked Simon Chandler the head of the National Security Agency, who was intrigued and worried that his agents had not heard a word about this program. He guessed that the President and the Secretary of State had secretly been working on the idea of an Ark without his agency being informed. It 'ruffled his feathers' that he had been passed over and not informed when he should have been informed, as it affected the security of the country.

"Well, we don't intend on building a boat," said the Secretary of State with a wry smile on his face, as a few chuckles and laughs echoed in the Oval Office before he continued with his answer. "Ark is just a word to describe the process by which we will try and save as much life as possible. For example, male and female animals of a species that can be located and easily breed in captivity will hopefully maintain their longevity. Eventually the off spring of these animals will be returned to their native lands and thereby start a new genesis. The flora will be saved by a seed repository. We will try and save as much as possible."

"We had to keep this program top secret, until, we were ready to inform those countries affected," interjected the President who could see that the NSA chief was mad. The President knew that Chandler wasn't an easy man to handle. The President saw the scrawl on the red faced Chandler and assumed he was more upset about being 'out of the loop' than any national security issue. The President remembered the first time they had met at his presidential inauguration ceremony and immediately took a dislike to the man. But, Simon Chandler was good at his job and he saw no reason to replace him as head of the NSA. The President had a belief that it was pointless to have people that only agreed with him.

"Please continue, Dom," said the President.

"Thanks, Mr. President. Are there any questions?"

"Yes, are there any other countries willing to participate in this Ark program?" asked the environment minister.

"Yes, there are and we hope more will join the effort as the program gets started. Currently Canada, Mexico, Brazil, Argentina and most of Latin America have expressed an interest in the program. The more countries that participate and we can coordinate their efforts then the greater the chance of saving more of the diversity of this planet."

"How can we be sure that our efforts to save life and diversity are not wasted in the possible panic that may ensue after the world hears the news about the coming catastrophe?" asked David Williams who had sat calmly throughout much of the meeting wondering if the decision by him and the other two conspirators had been the right choice.

"As you probably know the Internet has been rife for weeks about rumours and conspiracies regarding a cataclysmic event. It has been difficult to keep the lid on this top secret event. Partly, because we had to inform certain countries, so secrecy was always in doubt. Currently, we have several people locked up to keep a lid on this story. But, after the President informs the world then these people locked up can be released without charges," replied Dominic Penn.

"Thank you again, Dom," interjected the President before continuing. "I plan to make a speech tonight and inform the world. If I can convince the public that we have everything in hand, and that everyone not just governments can play a part in saving the planet then I hope that we can pull through this."

"Can we be certain of where the cosmic gamma rays will strike the Earth?" asked the environment minister.

"Yes, the scientists and number crunchers have been on this problem for weeks and they have been double checking their results over and over again. In fact, we have had a number of scientists working on the data. As you know the alien Iron Smart originally gave us the date and time and where the rays would strike the Earth. We are lucky in one sense that the Earth is dominated by seas. The Earth is three quarters sea and the rest land. Because of this the cosmic rays will strike mainly water," replied Dr. Gupta.

"What about the financial markets how will they react to this news?" asked the Treasury Secretary who had listened intently throughout the meeting wondering how the stock market would react? He had assumed that the markets would crash on the news and then bounce back after the market calculated the cost. He had already sold most of his stock portfolio when he had been informed by an insider of what was going to happen. The Treasury Secretary who had spent many years working for a leading financial organization before taking a position at the Treasury Department knew the markets and how they operated. It was a cut and thrust business where information was key to staying ahead in the game. The whole stock market ran on information where insider information could be gleaned from the actions of others. It was how the mathematical algorithms that constantly had an eye on the stock market worked. He was younger than most of the people at the meeting and he always looked immaculate with his Latin looks and dark brown hair, which he liked to apply some wax because he felt it made him look younger.

"Surely that's your department, Charlie," replied Dominic Penn the Secretary of State who was puzzled by the question.

"It was rhetorical, Dom. It is something we have discussed before in this room. I know the report I presented to this cabinet and the President speculated on different scenarios and what would be the likely costs. I just hope we are right and we don't have a complete breakdown of law and order and a complete collapse of the financial system. I know we have put in place certain money restrictions should that happen, but I cannot help worrying about the situation."

"It will have to work, otherwise, our civilisation will go back to the Stone Age," said Dominic Penn.

"Okay, lets wrap the meeting up for now," interjected the President who was conscious of the time and wanted to start phoning the heads of state and informing them of the coming catastrophe before his prime time speech later that day.

***

Charlie Sorkin got the nick name 'Blackbeard' because of his dark looks and his black and grey beard that was well groomed, which often under the beard disguised his emotions. As the Treasury Secretary to the President his job generally regarded the economic security of the United States of America.

That morning before the cabinet meeting at the White House the encrypted message had arrived from Frank Santoli. Frank had conveyed the message from Iron Smart to be read by the President. The message was brief and to the point. The message outlined the plan the aliens were willing to employ. The message from Iron Smart had to be broadcast to the world. The message had to mention that Iron Smart and the aliens were willing to help save the world. If the message was not broadcast then Iron Smart and their spacecraft would land on the lawn outside the White House. It was up to the President to make the decision.

Frank Santoli had given the President in the message background information to confirm the legitimacy of the message.

It was now up to Charlie Sorkin to decrypt the message and pass it on to the President without anyone else knowing about its existence. As Charlie Sorkin handed the President a report on the economic conditions favoured by the existence of the catastrophe, he carefully slipped the message for the President's eyes only on top of the report.

"What's this?" asked the President who was surprised to see the message had a coded title. Frank Santoli had devised the title. It would help the President realize its importance.

"It's a message from Iron Smart," replied Charlie Sorkin with his eyes firmly fixed on the President. He wondered if the President had remembered the alien.

As the President opened the envelope containing the message and began to read its contents, Charlie saw how the message had brought the President's attention almost immediately. The crease of wrinkles that crossed the President's face had grown and he now looked ten years older within seconds.

"This is good news, although, I'm not sure how the world will react?" said the President showing signs of stress as perspiration had started to form on his brow.

"Yes, Mr. President, but it is good news for the planet. Now, we have a chance to save the planet," replied Charlie Sorkin.

"I was planning to inform the world, today. Now, it's even more urgent. And, yes, we have a chance and they are willing to help. I will run their plan over with the scientists, just to see what they think. But, whatever way you shake it, we have no other choice," said the President.

"This Frank Santoli is quite a man and perhaps deserves a medal at some convenient point."

"Yes, Mr. President. We have been friends for many years. He is one of the straightest guys I know."

"This report on the economic effects of this catastrophe will help me make further decisions," said the President.

The President explained to Charlie Sorkin that his recent stock market activities had been monitored and that the President was aware of his behaviour. The President told Charlie that he had not fired him because of this behaviour up to now; because of the effect this may cause the stock market. But, the President said he would in time, when the time was right. He also mentioned there were others in the government that had been caught selling their stocks and shares. These people would also face the door at some time in the future.

"I'm glad Frank Santoli is an honest guy," the President remarked as he stared into the shocked eyes of Charlie Sorkin. Charlie had thought no one would find out about his shady dealing in the stock market.

"Yes, Mr. President."

"There are no exceptions. You will have to face those demons at a later date."

"I don't know what came over me. I should have known better. I felt I had to try and save my wealth. I know it was wrong. And, I am prepared for whatever happens," replied Charlie Sorkin.

The President gazed at Charlie Sorkin from behind his desk in the Oval Office with sorrow. Charlie Sorkin had been a competent treasury secretary. Now, Charlie looked like a child being scolded for bad behaviour. The President and Charlie were good friends, but this dishonesty had to be punished at some time, but now, was not the time or place. As Charlie made his way out of the Oval Office, he wondered about his future. What would his friend Frank Santoli think about his stock market dealings?

"Don't worry Charlie, we will work something out later," said the President.

"Thank you Mr. President."

"Thank you for all your recent efforts. My decisions are already made for me," said the President.

***

Later that day, the President of the United States had called for an urgent meeting with his cabinet in the Oval Office after receiving the decrypted message from Frank Santoli. Most of the cabinet were unaware of the recent news. Charlie Sorkin the Treasury Secretary watched the President as he unfolded the piece of paper on his desk with the coded text message containing the demands the alien Iron Smart had made. Sorkin noticed the President looked a different man a much younger man with the worry of the world behind him.

There was a hush in the room. The cabinet members sat in silence eager to know what had changed since the previous cabinet meeting earlier that day. You would have been able to hear a needle pin drop it was that quiet as everyone waited for the President to speak.

"I will be announcing to the world, tonight, about the catastrophe and about how we have a plan to save the world," said the President to the members of the cabinet who were stunned by the news. The cabinet had reconciled themselves to the coming apocalypse like the fate of men and women on death's row.

"What is your plan?" asked David Williams head of the CIA who was now intrigued to know why the President looked so jolly. Williams had noticed the deep wrinkles on the President's face had now faded and been replaced by the glow of a cheerful face like someone arriving back from a relaxing sunshine holiday.

"It's not my plan, but the alien Iron Smart's plan," replied the President who looked confident for the first time in many months.

The president read the message to the cabinet and its conditions. He also carefully read out the plan for the United States. This is the only available option that we have. How the public will react is anyone's guess. I will have our scientists look at Iron Smart's plan, but we have no other choice. The President explained all the details of the alien's plan, but refused to say how he received the message. I'm hoping that the alien will allow some of our scientists' access to their spacecraft to observe and help in defending the planet. We can only hope that the aliens have good intentions."

"I hope you are right, Mr. President," interjected David Williams head of the CIA.

Chapter 11

The three government security directors were gathered at a safe house close to the Capital. The safe house was a former underground storage facility that was well managed by the CIA.

"The issue is closed," said David Williams director of the CIA.

"Oh, by the way... that paper on how to find the unexpected. I remembered, it's by Padmanabhan and Tuzhilin, 1999."

David Williams explained the paper on artificial intelligence was by Padmanabhan and Tuzhilin, 1999, and stressed the importance of the outlier, which he had mentioned before on how to find the fugitives that they were seeking. Williams explained that artificial intelligence will only take you so far. If you fail to take notice of the outlier then anything is possible.

Williams said, "If you do not expect it, you will not find the unexpected, for it is hard to find and difficult." Pausing for a moment, before continuing, he said, "This was a quote from the paper that helped in locating the original paper on artificial intelligence."

"I will take a look," said Jeremy Katz head of the Department of Homeland Security.

"Yes, I will also," said Simon Chandler head of the National Security Agency.

"It's up to the aliens to save the day, otherwise, we are fried," said Katz who was only stating the obvious.

"We cannot be absolutely sure where on Earth the cosmic gamma rays will hit. We may have miss-calculated, somehow...shit happens," said Williams.

"Shit, always happens...when had a plan worked first time?" said Katz who was conscious of the military missions that never went to plan. He had the scars to prove it, he said to himself.

Pouring a drink from the well-stocked bar, Williams said, "Whatever happens the aliens are the fall guys? We had no part in it. The WR104 protocol never existed. Our meetings never took place."

***

The months had passed and finally the week had arrived when the cosmic gamma ray would hit the Earth. A week earlier Frank Santoli, Professor Aaron Mikovitz, Dr. Janet Taylor and Dr. Phoebe Gupta had been allowed to travel to the mother ship to witness what the aliens were about to do to save the planet. The President had insisted that Dr. Phoebe Gupta accompany Frank Santoli and the others to the mother ship as a witness to the technology the aliens were planning to use against the cosmic gamma rays.

Before boarding the spacecraft that had landed in a clearing surrounded by forest close to Washington D.C. the President thanked Frank Santoli, Professor Aaron Mikovitz, Dr. Janet Taylor and Dr. Phoebe Gupta for their service to their country. Frank had arranged the meeting with Iron Smart and their travel to the mother ship.

As the four of them climbed the ramp up into the spacecraft Iron Smart was waiting at the door to greet them. Frank took a brief look back to see the President and his security personal get into an unmarked car. He wondered what was in store for him and his colleagues.

"Greetings," said Iron Smart in his usual metallic sounding voice that almost could echo to the humans' ears.

"Greetings to you," replied Frank Santoli as he watched his colleagues greet the alien. It had been nearly two years since he first saw the alien spacecraft in Mongolia. A lot had happened since then. The world had got used to the reality of aliens. Although, some people refused to believe in aliens, even when the government had announced their presence on Earth. The aliens were here to help humanity and the planet, but some people still would not believe. The doubters didn't trust the aliens. Frank also had doubts about the motives of the aliens, but humanity had no other choices but to accept their help.

As the spacecraft blasted off from the Earth and into space, Frank Santoli and his colleagues saw the blue planet against the blackness of space for the first time. Frank's thoughts turned to the aliens' technology and how it surpassed what humanity at present could do. He could not feel any 'g force' on his body and wondered how the aliens had accomplished that problem? Sat beside his colleagues, he watched on a large screen that was part of the wall in the control room as the spacecraft approached the mothership. Frank saw that the mother ship was huge. He estimated that it was probably about one mile long and a half a mile high. The mother ship's structure was like a series of tower blocks laid on one side with circular towers added to the structure. Frank counted at least six circular towers along the length of the structure. It had a series of what looked like cone shaped exhaust systems that were as big as freight containers. He counted eight exhaust pipes as large as a freight lorry. The whole structure would take someone at least several weeks or more to explore, he mused.

"What do you think?" asked Frank as he turned to Aaron who was sat beside him.

"It's impressive and let's hope their technology can avert a catastrophe on Earth," replied Aaron in awe of the size of the mother ship and the aliens' technology.

They all watched as the shuttle spacecraft they were in adjusted to land on a protruding platform, before entering the mothership. As the platform moved the shuttle spacecraft into the mothership the spacecraft's outer air was equalized to the pressure inside the mothership. The huge docking area was as large as a football field, thought Aaron. As Frank, Aaron, Janet and Phoebe followed Iron Smart down the shuttle spacecraft's ramp onto the docking area they all saw a number of spacecraft being worked on by aliens. Aaron counted eight spacecraft in the docking area with room for more, Aaron thought.

Aaron thoughts turned to what Iron Smart had said previously about the evolution of man. He would ask again, what the alien knew. When the time was right, he would find out what the alien knew. It had been bugging his mind, since the day the alien had mentioned that we were wrong about the evolution of man. He was determined to find out the truth, he said to himself.

Following Iron Smart they all sat aboard a suspended vehicle that hovered above the floor. It reminded Frank of the hover trains he had experienced in Japan. This vehicle also ran along a track suspended by magnetic distraction, allowing the vehicle to move without wheels or the need for power. Iron Smart had explained that the energy came from the magnetic distraction, which powered the vehicle forward along the track.

"This is similar to what we have on Earth," said Aaron happily glad to compare the aliens' technology with what humans had to offer.

"Yes, the Japanese have this type of technology," announced Janet.

"It's just they are much more advanced than we are," retorted Phoebe.

"Just look at the size of this spacecraft…it's colossal," interjected Frank.

"We would struggle to build anything this size in space," retorted Phoebe.

"Phoebe, have you had any thoughts on the energy required to deflect the cosmic gamma rays?" asked Frank.

"It's a problem, I have been working on it in my mind ever since we were invited here," replied Phoebe.

"Do you have any ideas?" chirped Janet who was keen to know what Phoebe thought.

"Yes, I do. But, that would be speculation. I really need to know what the energy of the force field is and compare that against the energy of the cosmic gamma rays? Once, I know that I can work out the likelihood of the mission to deflect the cosmic rays. It's all down to mathematics and gravitational forces," replied Phoebe.

As the hover vehicle propelled itself along the track it made no noise it was as if the vehicle was switched off and stationary, thought Frank. He could see why the hover vehicle was necessary on such a large spacecraft. The vehicle came to a halt inside what looked like the main control room for the spacecraft, thought Aaron, he then saw numerous aliens attending to devices, which looked like computer terminals that were holographical to the eyes. As Iron Smart and the four of them disembarked from the hover vehicle, Iron Smart spoke in a language to the aliens that Aaron and his companions could not understand. Aaron noticed the control room was much like the shuttle spacecraft's control room. On each wall of the room, Aaron noticed large visual screens, which were part of the fabric of the wall.

"Commander, our force field is fully operational," said Shogi with its metallic voice echoing the control room like a musical note.

"We now have the force field deployed," said Iron Smart as its eyes displayed the color green then back to black as it spoke.

"Are you certain this force field will deflect the cosmic gamma rays?" asked Dr. Phoebe Gupta.

"We have been testing the force field, it will deflect any radiation it comes into contact with," replied Iron Smart in a metallic tone of voice with no emotion.

"Can I ask, what is the energy of the force field?" asked Dr. Phoebe Gupta.

"Why do you ask?" asked Iron Smart.

"I would like to know so I can work out how effective the force field will be," replied Phoebe.

"I will instruct Shogi to show you. You will find that we have enough energy deployed to deflect all the radiation. We are only able to protect Earth; everything else will be hit by the cosmic gamma rays. Any life in the solar system will be annihilated by the radiation," said Iron Smart.

"How is the force field generated?" asked Dr. Phoebe Gupta.

"I will instruct Shogi to show you," replied Iron Smart.

"Why are you so eager to save our planet," asked Frank Santoli.

"We have told you that life is abundant in the universe and intelligent life is rare," replied Iron Smart.

"It's seems too good to be true," chirped Janet rhetorically.

"Look!"

As the alien points with one arm to a visual screen above their heads, Iron Smart said, "Watch as the nuclear missile explodes on the force field. No radiation travels through the force field. You can see the Electro Magnetic Pulse (EMP) force is also deflected. We are locked in orbit like your moon is locked to your planet. Our force field is deployed like a triangle of a pyramid. From the apex it expands out to cover the Earth. This is how we can cover the Earth and safe guard life. We are at the correct distance from Earth and from this point we can deploy our force field to deflect all radiation and any EMPs."

"How do you generate the energy for the force field?" asked Dr. Phoebe Gupta who was by now relentless in her eagerness to learn as much as she could from the aliens.

"We use the element we call stardium 185. This element generates the force field, which is like what you see by way of magnetic attraction on Earth. The particles of atoms are forced to attract to each other and behave much like magnets on Earth do," replied Iron Smart.

"This stardium 185, what is it?" asked Dr. Phoebe Gupta.

"Stardium 185 is an alloy containing several different metals, mainly what you call aluminium and the element stardium 185. We harvest stardium 185 from the stars."

"I will have to see this element for myself," replied Dr. Phoebe Gupta.

"You're not the only one," stated Janet.

"We have had the force field in place for many days, since the start of my mission. My mission is to save the planet from destruction," said Iron Smart.

***

The day had finally arrived, when humanity would know if it had avoided a catastrophe of Biblical proportions or not. Frank Santoli and his three colleagues would have a 'bird's eye view' from gazing at the giant visual screen in the control room of the alien's mother ship.

Iron Smart the commander of the alien mother ship had already given orders to the humans to wear a special space suit designed to protect them from any radiation that may get through the force field, it would act like the magnetic force field protecting Earth. Iron Smart and the other aliens needed no special space suit because they were not biological entities they were only artificial intelligent robots. The humans on board the mother ship were in the middle between the force field protecting the mother ship and the Earth's own magnetic force field. The radiation from the cosmic gamma rays would be travelling at the speed of light and could destroy the DNA structure within the human body without the extra protection of the special space suits.

The whole event would only last a few seconds, enough time to wipe out fifty percent of the biological and ecological diversity on planet Earth. The force field generated by the mother ship to protect Earth from the cosmic gamma rays would stay in place for several months to allow the passing of another wave of highly radiated particles due after the main cosmic gamma rays had passed by.

The second wave of dangerous radiation although not travelling as fast as the first cosmic gamma rays they still had the capacity to inflect serious damage to humans over a longer period of time. Instead of dying within seconds to days from the first wave of rays the second wave would manifest itself over a period of years. People would be susceptible to getting cancer such as leukaemia.

A Space Time Apocalypse

As they all gazed at the screen on the wall, which showed an animation of the event taking place they saw how the force field deflected the incoming cosmic gamma rays. They saw the force field, which projected out from the mother ship forming a cone like structure with the widest end protecting the mother ship and the Earth below.

"You can see how the force field is deflecting the gamma rays away from the Earth," announced Dr. Phoebe Gupta to her colleagues through the communication device inside the space suit.

"Yes, it's amazing and it seems to be working…thank God," said Dr. Janet Taylor who was relieved that the force field was working.

"If any radiation gets through the force field it will be considerably slower and therefor our own magnetic force field will deflect the rest to the poles," remarked Dr. Phoebe Gupta.

"I hope you are right?" asked Frank Santoli rhetorically.

"I have done the calculations and everything seems to be normal. We have a good chance all of this is going to work. At least humanity will be saved, until the next time it happens. We may not have the help of the aliens the next time we have a similar event," replied Dr. Phoebe Gupta.

The hour had arrived when the two second event would capture everyone's attention. As Aaron watched the animation on the large screen on the wall it reminded him of a wave of water crashing down on a large boulder on the sea shore. The animations showed how the force field was like the boulder deflecting everything around it to its sides. As the cosmic gamma rays hit the force field the rays were deflected harmlessly away from Earth.

"The force field is holding up," announced Aaron to his colleagues as their attention was glued to the visual screen like bees to a honey comb.

"Look!" shouted Dr. Janet Taylor as she pointed with one arm to the screen where the force field was failing.

"Why is it failing?" asked Dr. Phoebe Gupta who was dumbfounded to why the force field was failing because she had made the calculations several times and had come to the conclusion that the force field would stand up to the cosmic gamma rays.

"Perhaps, you made a mistake," replied Frank Santoli gazing at Dr. Phoebe Gupta for an answer.

"If these cosmic gamma rays get to Earth they will cause untold damage," said Aaron as he watched the animation disintegrate more and more as the cosmic gamma rays slammed straight into the force field.

Iron Smart said, "Do not worry. We have planned for this to happen. It's just the intensity of the gamma rays hitting the stardium 185 particles. The cosmic gamma rays have been slowed down by the particles in the force field causing a release of energy, which is what you are seeing on the screen. The particles in the force field bend the cosmic gamma ray particles around the force field forcing the gamma rays to slow down enough so that the rays can be harmlessly deflected away from Earth."

"I was worried that I had made the wrong calculations," retorted Dr. Gupta as the mother ship started to shake.

"It will be all over in a few seconds," announced Iron Smart as the giant robot swayed with the shaking of the mother ship.

As Aaron stood holding on to Janet he made a promise to himself. He had to find out what the alien meant about the evolution of man. It had been bugging him ever since Iron Smart had said that our understanding about the evolution of man was wrong. He had gone out of his way to speak to Dr. Helen Baring about her theory on the evolution of man. But, he felt there was more and the alien knew the truth and he was determined to find the truth, he said to himself.

"The cosmic gamma rays have passed," announced Iron Smart as its green eyes flashed on and off.

"That's it then, we can go home," retorted Frank as he raised his hands in the air in jubilation.

"My mission is not over," said Dr. Gupta.

"What do you mean?" asked Aaron.

"I need to understand as much of their technology as I can," replied Dr. Gupta.

"My mission is not over," said Iron Smart to the humans.

"The force field will need to be regenerated," said Shogi to its commander Iron Smart.

"Yes, restart the process and prepare for the next wave of radiation!" instructed Iron Smart to his second in command, Shogi.

Iron Smart explained to the humans that the mother ship would stay in orbital lock with Earth, until the second wave of radiation had passed. Iron Smart showed the humans on a visual screen how the second wave of radiation would be deflected away from Earth. The process of generating a force field strong enough to deflect the radiation would take a considerable amount of power. Iron Smart explained the power would come from helium 3 mined on the moon. The substance helium 3 would be transported by shuttle spacecraft to the mother ship, until the mother ship had enough power to generate the force field required to deflect the second wave of radiation.

Aaron remembered reading about helium 3 ever since the early Apollo missions to the moon. Apparently, the moon has an abundant supply of helium 3, whereas the substance was relatively rare on Earth, he had read. The substance helium 3 was an excellent power source, because of its ability to move atoms. Helium 3 was like uranium used in nuclear power stations on Earth without the harmful radiation. Also, it was in plentiful supply on the moon and close to the surface, so it was easy to mine. The element Helium 3 was made by the fusion nuclear reaction of the Sun that made the photons particles we experience as sunlight on Earth.

"Can I ask you a question, Iron Smart?" asked Aaron as he climbed out of the space suit he had been made to wear against any radiation getting through to the mother ship.

"Yes, go ahead."

"What did you mean about the evolution of man? You said that we had it all wrong," asked Aaron waiting for a comprehensive answer as his colleagues listened into the conversation.

"Have you asked yourself why your astronauts in space have a rhythm that reverts to a cycle that conforms exactly to the cycle of Mars? This cycle is called the Circadian rhythm," replied Iron Smart

"No, I didn't know this," retorted Aaron.

"Yes, I have heard about this anomaly," announced Dr Gupta.

"Perhaps, you will explain?" asked Iron Smart.

Dr. Gupta explained to her colleagues about how astronauts in zero gravity in space revert to this particular rhythm. It is called the Circadian rhythm because it derives from the Greek word for cycle. The Circadian rhythm is your body clock, which helps to regulate your sleep and wake cycle. She explained that all biological organisms exhibit this behaviour. Dr. Gupta said the rotation of Mars around the sun is approximately twenty four hours and thirty seven minutes, whereas the rotation of the Earth as it goes round the Sun is approximately twenty three hours and fifty six minutes. The anomaly is not well understood; therefor, scientists tend to find reasons why it should be the case. Dr. Gupta explained to her colleagues why she thought the anomaly existed. She explained that at some time in the past, she postulated that the Earth must have had a rotation the same as the present rotation of Mars and this is why astronauts reverted to this rhythm in space.

"Otherwise, why would our astronauts and their internal body clock's revert to the Circadian rhythm of Mars in zero gravity?" said Dr. Gupta.

"But, this doesn't answer my question about the evolution of man," retorted Aaron.

"Think for a while. You may already know the answer to your question, Aaron," replied Iron Smart with its metallic tone of voice.

"Are you saying, we came from Mars," stated Dr. Janet Taylor.

"Think about why your young rely on their mothers for a long time. If you evolved on the savanna in Africa then why have other animals born on the savanna have the ability to immediately walk and run? Don't forget you are just another animal," replied Iron Smart.

"So, you are inferring that man didn't evolve on this planet?" asked Frank Santoli.

"Yes, that is correct," retorted Iron Smart.

Iron Smart continued and explained to the humans that millions of years ago a nuclear explosion destroyed the atmosphere on Mars. Leaving my masters no choice, they had to move to another planet. A colony was sent to your planet and the rest went to the stars.

"What caused the nuclear explosion?" asked Frank.

"The planet Mars was attacked by another intelligent alien life force," replied Iron Smart.

"Why were you attacked by this alien life force?" asked Dr. Gupta.

"Because our technology was a threat to their existence," replied Iron Smart.

"Could this alien life force attack Earth?" asked Aaron who was now anxious to know the answer.

"Yes, if your technology becomes advanced enough that it threatens their existence," replied Iron Smart.

"How would we know when that happens? I mean what level of technology?" asked Dr. Taylor.

"When you can travel between the stars," replied Iron Smart.

Iron Smart explained that its masters had the technology to travel between the stars and sent spacecraft on missions to survey the stars. It was on one of these missions to the stars when the spacecraft never returned. It was assumed the spacecraft crash landed somewhere or broke up in space. Iron Smart explained that the spacecraft stopped sending signals in an area you call Orion's Belt.

"So, your masters are us is that what you want us to believe?" retorted Frank.

"Yes, that is correct," replied Iron Smart.

"What proof have you?" enquired Dr. Gupta.

"I have already told you," countered Iron Smart.

***

The following day Frank Santoli, Professor Aaron Mikovitz, Dr. Janet Taylor and Dr. Phoebe Gupta had arrived back on Earth to give their report to the President of the United States of America. As the four of them sat in the Oval Office in front of the seated President they waited for the President to speak.

"So, please tell me what you experienced?" asked the President.

"You have my written report, Mr. President," responded Dr. Phoebe Gupta who had been keen for the President to read it.

"Yes, I have not had time to read it. Please give me a verbal brief," said the President.

Dr. Gupta explained to the President that the mission to save the planet had been successful. This was achieved she explained by the use of a force field generated by the alien's mothership. The mothership was enormous as large as several football fields and at least as wide and high as the Empire State building. She explained that the mothership had been parked on the dark side of the moon. Currently, the mothership is locked in orbit around the Earth to protect it from more radiation expected to arrive in the next few weeks, she explained.

"When will we know we are safe from this supernova?" asked the President.

"When the last of the highly radiated particles have passed Earth, we then expect a message from the alien Iron Smart," replied Dr. Gupta.

"Please, continue with your brief," said the President.

Dr. Gupta continued her brief to the President outlining what happened during the impact with the cosmic gamma rays.

"Thank you, Dr. Gupta for your brief. Would you like to give your experience, Professor Aaron Mikovitz?" asked the President.

"Yes, there is more. During my contact with the alien Iron Smart, I was intrigued by what the alien said about the evolution of man. Iron Smart had said that we were wrong about the evolution of man. I was intrigued enough to speak to a leading anthropologist Dr. Helen Baring at the Berkeley university in California about her theory on the evolution of man. Dr. Baring and other leading scientists contend that a special event occurred around forty to fifty thousand years ago. They postulate that around this time man began to paint on cave walls and also developed sophisticated tools not seen before in our archaeological record. Dr Baring said that for a million years man had used stone tools that had hardly changed in that time, yet, suddenly, man had developed abstract thought and probably language overnight in terms of the archaeological record."

"Sorry to interrupt you, Professor, but I have other engagements and would like to hear what Dr. Taylor and Frank Santoli have to say before we conclude this meeting. I would like you, Dr. Taylor and Mr. Santoli to submit a report of your findings and experience to this office as soon as possible," remarked the President.

"Of course, Mr. President," replied Aaron.

"What is your experience Dr. Taylor?" asked the President.

"Much of it has already been said. In fact, we were all present when Aaron asked the alien Iron Smart for proof about the evolution of man. What Iron Smart said makes logical sense, but I have my doubts. Perhaps, when I have filed my report you will see what I mean. Until then I will let Mr. Santoli speak," replied Dr. Taylor.

"Okay, what are your thoughts, Mr Santoli?" asked the President.

"I concur with what has already been said. We were told by the alien possibly what they wanted us to believe. Iron Smart said that their planet what we call Mars was hit by a nuclear explosion, which striped the planet of its atmosphere. The alien said that a colony was sent to our planet Earth and the rest went to the stars to search for a new home. We were told by Iron Smart that an alien life force sent the nuclear bombs to Mars because they were seen as a threat to their existence. We were told that Earth would be a target for destruction if we developed technology to enable us to travel to the stars."

"Can all this be verified?" asked the President.

"I don't know?" replied Frank Santoli.

"A nuclear explosion caused by the signature of a nuclear bomb has been verified in the atmosphere of Mars. The presence of xenon one hundred twenty nine in the atmosphere can only be caused by a nuclear bomb," interjected Dr. Gupta.

"Okay, I wait for your reports," responded the President.

***

Several weeks later, Frank Santoli was busy in his apartment preparing a meal for Phoebe. His love affair with Dr. Phoebe Gupta had begun aboard the alien mother ship several weeks earlier. Frank saw Phoebe on the external CCTV waiting for him to buzz her into the apartment block. As Frank waited for Phoebe to climb the stairs to his second floor apartment, he then realized what he needed to do. It had been on his mind, ever since, being reinstated by order of the President with his old job at the CIA. Frank held Phoebe tightly in his arms and with passion kissed her cherry color lips for several minutes before whispering in her ear, "I can say a thousand words, but only three that count, I love you."

"Do you really mean that and why are you whispering?" asked Phoebe.

"Yes, I mean it and because you are standing in the hall way and I don't want to wake the old lady that lives in the apartment opposite," stressed Frank.

"Please, come in!"

"I can smell you're cooking. What is it?"

"Chicken *tikka masala* and *basmati* rice."

As Frank took hold of Phoebe with one hand and led her into his apartment, he said, "Will you marry me?"

With a cute smile she replied, "Let me see what your cooking is like first." Pausing for moment she continued, "Of course, I will."

"Great, let's eat and celebrate."

Toasting their proposal with a glass of *Brunello di Montalcino* a compliment to the food, Frank said, "I have decided to retire from the CIA. Working for the CIA is not a job for a future married man."

Chapter 12

As I sat there at my desk, it felt different; time had a way of making things last longer than they actually take. It appeared, as if time had stopped for what looked like about ten minutes; yet, time on the clock on my desk seemed still the same. But, there was something different about the day. It almost felt like time had indeed stopped for a short time almost like Déjà vu where you feel you have experienced the moment and place before somehow, yet, you haven't been to the place as far as you know it. As I write this journal for humanity, I hope it finally ends up in the right hands; otherwise, man's struggle with the aliens when they landed was futile as they were like zombies and what happened in the following years was buried in the dust of the carnage that followed...

Commander S.S. Gupta, Mars Project, April 27th 2069

www.ingramcontent.com/pod-product-compliance
Ingram Content Group UK Ltd.
Pitfield, Milton Keynes, MK11 3LW, UK
UKHW021323180426
11947UKWH00017B/1397